# Problem Solving Study Guide

to accompany

# Mathematics
# for
# Elementary Teachers

## A CONTEMPORARY APPROACH
### Third Edition

## Gary L. Musser
## William F. Burger
Oregon State University
Corvallis, OR

Prepared by
# Don Miller
St. Cloud State University
St. Cloud, MN

Macmillan College Publishing Company
New York
Maxwell Macmillan Canada
Toronto
Maxwell Macmillan International
New York   Oxford   Singapore   Sidney

Macmillan College Publishing Company
866 Third Avenue, New York, New York 10022

Macmillan College Publishing Company is part of the
Maxwell Communications Group of Companies.

Maxwell Macmillan Canada, Inc.
1200 Eglinton Avenue East, Suite 200
Don Mills, Ontario M3C 3N1

ISBN   0-02-381304-0

Printing:  1 2 3 4 5 6 7 8     Year:  4 5 6 7 8 9 0 1 2 3

# PREFACE

The purpose of this study guide is to provide preservice and inservice elementary and middle school teachers with non-routine problem solving experiences to help them become better problem solvers. Knowing when and how to apply a variety of strategies will, in turn, provide teachers with techniques that they can use in teaching problem solving in mathematics.

Each of the twenty-one sections in this study guide consist of four pages, which includes the following components.

### Strategy

Each section begins by introducing a strategy along with a problem to be analyzed by students individually or in small groups. The purpose of the opening problem is to introduce a particular strategy. Students should initially attempt to solve the problem by applying the given strategy even though an alternate strategy may, at times, seem more natural. Later, alternate approaches to solving problems will be encouraged. These initial pages have been designed to serve as overhead masters.

### Solution

A solution to the opening problem is provided on the top of second page of each section. At first, these solutions are quite complete. However, as students progress through this book, they are asked to provide missing portions of the solutions. Also included are some questions related to the problem, a discussion of the strategy, and a list of clues suggesting when the strategy may be appropriate in solving a problem.

### Practice Problems

The purpose here is to provide students with an opportunity to practice solving problems by applying this section's strategy.

### Mixed Strategy Practice

Each section ends with a set of four problems that can be solved by using one or more of the strategies which have been introduced up to that point. After students have had ample time to analyze the problems, a discussion with students about their approaches should be very beneficial.

In addition to these sections, there are 42 additional practice problems and 56 additional mixed strategy problems. Answers for odd-numbered problems are found at the end of this study guide and answers to the even-numbered problems are contained in the Instructor's Manual for *Mathematics for Elementary Teachers - A Contemporary Approach* by Gary L. Musser and William F. Burger.

The problem solving strategies illustrated in this study guide are identical to those presented in the textbook *Mathematics for Elementary Teachers - A Contemporary Approach*. Thus, this study guide may be used in conjunction with the Musser/Burger textbook to provide students with additional non-routine problem solving experiences. In addition, this guide can serve to supplement any mathematics education course or workshop for elementary or middle school teachers where improving skills in problem solving is a main goal.

I wish to thank and commend Marilyn Wallace, Julie Borden, Sue Borden, and Bishnu Naraine for their expert word processing and Ron Bagwell for his creative artwork. I also wish to thank Gary Musser and Bill Burger for sharing their problem solving strategy clues with me for use in this book.

Don Miller

# CONTENTS

# Guess and Test

Tom and Barb have only nickels and dimes. Barb has 75 cents and Tom has 90 cents. Both have the same number of coins and Tom has the same number of dimes as Barb has nickels. How many nickels does Barb have?

## SOLUTION

Problem:   Tom and Barb have only nickels and dimes.  Barb has 75 cents and Tom has 90 cents.  Both have the same number of coins and Tom has the same number of dimes as Barb has nickels.  How many nickels does Barb have?

Solution:   Barb must have an odd number of nickels.  Why?  Barb and Tom have the same number of coins.  The number of Barb's nickels equals the number of Tom's dimes.

|  | 75¢ Barb | | 90¢ Tom | | |
|---|---|---|---|---|---|
|  | N | D | N | D |  |
| Guess | ⑨ | 3 | 0 | ⑨ | $9 + 3 \neq 0 + 9$ |
| Guess | ⑤ | 5 | 8 | ⑤ | $5 + 5 \neq 8 + 5$ |
|  | ⋮ | ⋮ | ⋮ | ⋮ |  |
| Guess | ⑦ | 4 | 4 | ⑦ | $7 + 4 = 4 + 7$ |

a.   This solution displays random guess and test.  Describe a systematic way of solving it.
b.   Before solving the problem, it was noted that Barb must have an odd number of nickels.  What conclusion can you draw about the number of nickels Tom has?  Explain.
c.   Explain how the information like that in part b is helpful in solving the problem.

## DISCUSSION

In using the Guess and Test strategy, the first step is to guess a possible answer to the question asked in the problem.  A test is then made to determine if your guess satisfies the conditions of the problem.  This process (guess and test) continues as you systematically try to improve your guesses until a solution is obtained.

## CLUES

The Guess and Test strategy may be appropriate when:

*    There is a limited number of possible answers to test.
*    You want to gain a better understanding of the problem.
*    You have a good idea of what the answer is.
*    You can systematically try possible answers.
*    Your choices have been narrowed down by the use of other strategies.
*    There is no other obvious strategy to try.

## PRACTICE PROBLEMS

| Problem: | It costs 29 cents to mail a letter and 19 cents to mail a postcard. Tina wrote to 20 people last month. Her cost for postage was $5.20. How many postcards did she write during that time? |
|---|---|

Solution:  Guess and Test

|  | 1st Guess | 2nd Guess | 3rd Guess | 4th Guess |
|---|---|---|---|---|
| Number of letters | 10 | 8 | 12 | 14 |
| Number of postcards | 10 | 12 | 8 | 6 |
| Postage | $4.80 | $4.60 | $5.00 | $5.20 |

Tina wrote  6  postcards and  14  letters.

1–A.  A rectangular field has a perimeter of 220 meters and an area of 2,856 square meters. What are its dimensions?

1–B.  The sum of two counting numbers is 91. Half of one number is three times the other number. What are the numbers?

# MIXED STRATEGY PRACTICE

**PROBLEM-SOLVING STRATEGIES**

| 1. Guess and Test |
| --- |

1-1. The numbers 1 through 16 can be placed in a 4×4 array so that the sum of each row and the sum of the four corner numbers are the same. Find the missing numbers in the figure shown below.

```
15    *    *    4
 *    3    *    5
 8    *    *   11
 1   12    *    *
```

1-2. Find the two counting numbers which have a difference of 21 and a product of 1,696.

1-3. Ken bought some pencils and erasers for $1.80. The erasers were 15 cents each and the pencils were 6 cents each. How many of each did he buy if he ended up with more erasers than pencils?

1-4. How can 7 trees be planted so that there are 6 rows of trees in a straight line with each row having 3 trees?

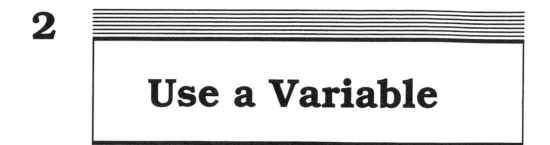

## Use a Variable

After the first two terms in the following sequence, each number is the sum of the preceding two terms. Find the missing numbers.

4 \_\_\_ \_\_\_ \_\_\_ \_\_\_ 67

## SOLUTION

Problem:  After the first two terms in the following sequence, each number is the sum of the preceding two terms. Find the missing numbers.

4 ___ ___ ___ ___ 67

Solution:  Let $x$ represent the second term of the sequence.

| 4 | $\underline{\phantom{xxx}}$ | $\underline{\phantom{xxx}}$ | $\underline{\phantom{xxx}}$ | $\underline{\phantom{xxx}}$ | 67 |
|---|---|---|---|---|---|
|   | $x$ | $x + 4$ | $2x + 4$ | $3x + 8$ | $5x + 12$ |

$$5x + 12 = 67 \longrightarrow x = 11$$

| Check: | 4 | $\underline{11}$ | $\underline{15}$ | $\underline{26}$ | $\underline{41}$ | 67 |
|---|---|---|---|---|---|---|
|   |   |   | $4 + 11$ | $11 + 15$ | $15 + 26$ | $26 + 41$ |

a.  This problem could have been solved using Guess and Test. Is the Use a Variable strategy preferable? Why or why not?

b.  What is it about this problem that suggests the Use a Variable strategy?

## DISCUSSION

The Use a Variable strategy is often helpful when Guess and Test appears to be too inefficient. Also, there are times when a variable must be used. For example, consider the following products of consecutive even numbers increased by 1:

$$2 \times 4 + 1 = 9 = 3^2 \qquad 6 \times 8 + 1 = 49 = 7^2 \qquad 10 \times 12 + 1 = 121 = 11^2$$

These three examples suggest that a square will result in each such case. Since there are infinitely many even numbers, a variable must be employed. Verify this conjecture for all possible even numbers as follows:

$$2N (2N + 2) + 1 = 4N^2 + 4N + 1 = (2N + 1)^2.$$

Thus, by using a variable, we have shown that this statement is true for all even numbers.

## CLUES

The Use a Variable strategy may be appropriate when:

* A phrase similar to "for any number" is present or implied.
* A problem suggests an equation.
* A proof or a general solution is required.
* A problem contains phrases such as "consecutive", "even", "odd", etc. whole numbers.
* There is a large number of cases.
* A proof is asked for in a problem involving numbers.
* There is an unknown quantity related to known quantities.
* There is an infinite number of numbers involved.
* You are trying to develop a general formula.

## PRACTICE PROBLEMS

---

Problem: The sum of two counting numbers is 91. Half of one number equals three times the other number. What are the numbers?

---

Solution: Use a Variable

Let $x$ and $y$ represent the two numbers.

The sum is 91: $\quad x + y = 91$

Half of one equals 3 times the other: $\quad \dfrac{x}{2} = 3y \qquad$ or $\quad x = 6y$

$x + y = 91$ and $x = 6y$ implies that $6y + y = 91$

Hence, $y = 13$ and $x = 78$.

This problem was presented earlier in the Guess and Test section. The solution above shows a more efficient way to solve the problem.

---

2-A. Tom has 9 more baseball cards than Ken and Jill has 3 less than Randy. If Randy has 4 more cards than Ken, could the total numbers of cards they have be 45?

2-B. Show that any six consecutive even whole numbers can be written in the figure so that the sum of the three numbers on each side of the triangle is the same.

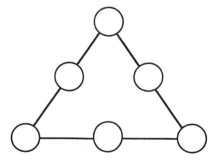

# MIXED STRATEGY PRACTICE

**PROBLEM-SOLVING STRATEGIES**

1. Guess and Test
2. Use a Variable

2-1. Find the whole number represented by the fraction below without actually doing the calculations involved.

$$\frac{67897652^2 - 67897651 \times 67897653 + 67897650}{67897651}$$

2-2. Bruce was a pupil at Madison Elementary School in 1945. The year of his birth is a perfect square. How old was he on his birthday in 1988?

2-3. Write any three counting numbers in the first 3 blank spaces shown below. Continue with five more numbers, each being the sum of the preceding 3 terms. The sum of your eight numbers should be equal to 4 times the seventh number. Show why this must always be true.

| _____ | _____ | _____ | _____ |
|---|---|---|---|
| 1 | 2 | 3 | 4 |

| _____ | _____ | _____ | _____ |
|---|---|---|---|
| 5 | 6 | 7 | 8 |

$H = C + T$

$L = 4C + 2T$

$\begin{cases} H = L - 35 \\ H = 4C + 2T - 35 \end{cases}$

$C + T = 4C + 2T - 35$

$\boxed{3C + T = 35}$ ⑪

2-4. In a group of cows and turkeys, the number of heads is 35 less than the number of legs. What is the largest number of cows that could be in this group of animals?

# 3

# Draw a Picture

The surface of Big Lake is 31 feet above the surface of Long Lake. Long Lake is half as deep as Big Lake and the bottom of Long Lake is 8 feet below the bottom of Big Lake. How deep is each lake?

## SOLUTION

Problem:   The surface of Big Lake is 31 feet above the surface of Long Lake.  Long Lake is half as deep as Big Lake and the bottom of Long Lake is 8 feet below the bottom of Big Lake.  How deep is each lake?

Solution:   Draw a Picture

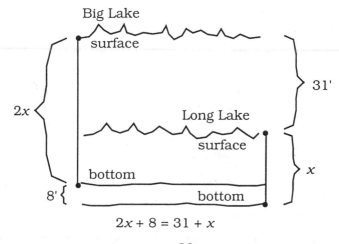

$$2x + 8 = 31 + x$$

$$x = 23$$

Big Lake is  46'  deep and Long Lake is  23'  deep.

a.  Convince yourself that the Draw a Picture strategy is helpful by trying to solve the problem without a picture.
b.  What is the depth of Clear Lake given that its surface is 10 feet below the surface of Big Lake and its bottom is 6 feet above the bottom of Long Lake?

## DISCUSSION

Many problems involve physical situations where the Draw a Picture strategy is helpful.  A picture provides a visual representation that usually leads to a better understanding of the problem.  This, in turn, often helps in devising a plan.

## CLUES

The Draw a Picture strategy may be appropriate when:

*   A physical situation is involved.
*   Geometric figures or measurements are involved.
*   You want to gain a better understanding of the problem.
*   A visual representation of the problem is possible.

## PRACTICE PROBLEMS

Problem:  A club has twenty rectangular tables that seat 3 people along each side and one person on each end.  These tables were placed end-to-end to form a long rectangular table.  How many people can be seated in this arrangement?  In general, how many people can be seated around *n* tables arranged in this way?

Solution:  Draw a Picture.

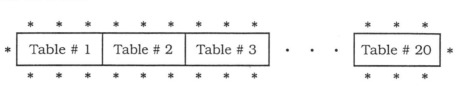

Sixty ($3 \times 20$) people can be seated along each side, one on each end.

Hence, 122 people can be seated at the long table. ($2 \times 60 + 2 \times 1 = 122$)

In general, $6n + 2$ people can be seated around *n* tables.

3–A.   A "Superbounce" ball rebounds half the height it drops.  The ball is dropped from a height of 176 feet.  How far off the ground is the ball when it has traveled a total of 500 feet?

3–B.   An office building has 33 floors, each 10 feet high, and elevators that travel at a constant speed.  If it takes 10 seconds for an elevator to go from the first floor to the fifth floor, how long will it take an elevator to go from the fifth floor to the middle floor?

# MIXED STRATEGY PRACTICE

PROBLEM-SOLVING
STRATEGIES

1. Guess and Test
2. Use a Variable
3. Draw a Picture

3–1. On a certain 20 question test, a student receives 4 points for each correct answer, loses 3 points for each incorrect answer, and loses 2 points if no answer is given. Todd took the test and scored 34 points. How many problems did he answer correctly?

3–2. Fencing is sold in 8 foot sections at $15 per section. Fence posts cost $4 each. How much will it cost to build a fence around a square field which is 240 feet on each side?

3–3. Is the sum of four consecutive counting numbers ever divisible by 4? If so, when? If not, why not?

3–4. Each day, Jason walks to his office at a constant rate. One-third of the way he passes a bank and three–fourths of the way to work he passes a store. At the bank his watch reads 6:52 A.M. and at the store it reads 7:02 A.M. At what time was Jason halfway to his office?

**4**

# Look for a Pattern

## How many beads are hidden under the cloud?

## SOLUTION

Problem:   How many beads are hidden under the cloud?

Solution:   What patterns do the black beads and white beads make?  What's hidden under the cloud; black beads, white beads, or some of both?

5 + 6 + 14 + 32 + 59 = 116

a.   Is Guess and Test appropriate for this problem?  Why or why not?
b.   Is the Use a Variable strategy helpful?  Why or why not?

## DISCUSSION

The Look for a Pattern strategy is often useful when a pattern is generated by systematically listing special cases of the problem.  For many problems, the pattern leads directly to the answer, while others will require further insight before a solution can be realized.

## CLUES

The Look for a Pattern strategy may be appropriate when:

*   A list of data is given.
*   A sequence or series of numbers is involved.
*   Listing special cases helps you deal with complex problems.
*   You are asked to make a prediction or generalization.
*   Information can be expressed and viewed in an organized manner, such as in a table.

## PRACTICE PROBLEMS

| | |
|---|---|
| Problem: | If the *s continue as shown below, what is the total number of *s that will be in sets R through T?<br>A: * *   B: * * * *   C: * * * * * *   D: * * * * * * * *   E: * * * * * * * * * *   . . . |

Solution:  Look for a Pattern

| A → 2 *s | B → 4 *s | C → 6 *s | D → 8 *s ... |
|---|---|---|---|

| 1 | 2 | 3 | 4 | 5 | 6 | | 18 | 19 | 20 |
|---|---|---|---|---|---|---|---|---|---|
| A | B | C | D | E | F | ... | R | S | T |
| 2 | 4 | 6 | 8 | 10 | 12 | ... | 36 | 38 | 40 |

The total number of *s in R, S, and T is 114 (36 + 38 + 40).

4–A.   If the *s continue as shown below, how many *s will be in set T?

```
A  * * *           B  * * * *         C  * * * * * *        D  * * * * * * *
   * *                * * * *            * * * * * *           * * * * * * *
                      * * * *            * * * * *             * * * * * * *
                                         * * * * *             * * * * * * *
                                                               * * * * * * *
                                                               * * * * * * *
```

4–B.   A  1  2  3      B  5  6  7      C  9  10  11      D  13  14  15

Use the pattern suggested above to help you find the missing terms.

a)  H  ____  ____  ____          b)  R  ____  ____  ____

c)  ____  ____  50  ____         d)  ____  ____  ____  63

e)  ____  ♣  ♥  ♠  where  ♣ + ♥ + ♠ = 258.

# MIXED STRATEGY PRACTICE

**PROBLEM-SOLVING STRATEGIES**

1. Guess and Test
2. Use a Variable
3. Draw a Picture
4. Look for a Pattern

4-1. Find the ones digit for each of the following.
Ones digit:

$3^1$ ___ $3^2$ ___ $3^3$ ___ $3^4$ ___

$3^5$ ___ $3^6$ ___ $3^7$ ___ $3^8$ ___

Predict the ones digit:

a. $3^{41}$ ___3___   b. $3^{63}$ ___7___

c. $4^{99}$ ___4___   d. $7^{98}$ ___9___

4-2. Each girl in a seventh grade class has as many pencils as there are girls and each boy has as many pencils as there are boys. There are 30 students with a total of 468 pencils. How many girls are in the class if there are more girls than boys?  18 G  12 B
18 x 18 + 12 x 12 = 468

4-3. Red (R) and white (W) balls are placed into boxes labeled Box #1, Box #2, Box #3, and so on. The arrangement of balls in each box is as follows:

| 1R 3W | 3R 6W | 5R 11W |
|-------|-------|--------|
| Box #1 | Box #2 | Box #3 |

W $N^2 + 2$

| 7R 18W | 9R 27W | 11R 38W |
|--------|--------|---------|
| Box #4 | Box #5 | Box #6 |

a. What is the total number of balls in box #29?
b. How many white balls are there in box #9?
c. What is the total number of red balls in the first 60 boxes?

4-4. Find the largest 5-digit perfect square that is divisible by 9.  99,925

# 5

# Make a List

I am thinking of three different whole numbers which have a product of 36. Five more than the sum of the numbers is a perfect square. What is the sum of my numbers?

## SOLUTION

Problem:   I am thinking of three different whole numbers that have a product of 36. Five more than the sum of the numbers is a perfect square. What is the sum of my numbers?

Solution:   The following list displays all possible triples of numbers whose product is 36.

| A | B | C | $A \cdot B \cdot C$ | $A + B + C$ | $A + B + C + 5$ |
|---|---|---|---|---|---|
| 1 | 1 | 36 | 36 | 38 | 43 |
| 1 | 2 | 18 | 36 | 21 | 26 |
| 1 | 3 | 12 | 36 | 16 | 21 |
| 1 | 4 | 9 | 36 | 14 | 19 |
| 1 | 6 | 6 | 36 | 13 | 18 |
| 2 | 2 | 9 | 36 | 13 | 18 |
| 2 | 3 | 6 | 36 | 11 | $\mathbf{16 = 4^2}$ |
| 3 | 3 | 4 | 36 | 10 | 15 |

$$2 + 3 + 6 = \underline{\underline{11}}$$

a.   Guess and Test could have been used to solve this problem. Is the Make a List strategy more efficient? Why or why not?
b.   Why is Use a Variable not an efficient strategy for this problem?

## DISCUSSION

An organized list sometimes leads directly to a solution or it may reveal a pattern that suggests a possible solution to the problem. For example, consider a list of all multiples of 99 between 1,000 and 2,000:

   1089   1188   1287   1386   1485   1584   1683   1782   1881   1980.

The list suggests that a 4-digit number A,BCD is a multiple of 99 when AB + CD = 99.

## CLUES

The Make a List strategy may be appropriate when:

*   Information can easily be organized and presented.
*   Data can easily be generated.
*   Listing the results obtained by using Guess and Test.
*   Asked "In how many ways" something can be done.
*   Trying to learn about a collection of numbers generated by a rule or formula.

## PRACTICE PROBLEMS

Problem: How many triangles of perimeter 12 inches are there if the length of each side must be a counting number?

Solution: Make a List

| X: | 1 | 1 | 1 | 1 | 1 | 2 | 2 | 2 | 2 | 3 | 3 | 4 |
|----|---|---|---|---|---|---|---|---|---|---|---|---|
| Y: | 1 | 2 | 3 | 4 | 5 | 2 | 3 | 4 | 5 | 3 | 4 | 4 |
| Z: | 10 | 9 | 8 | 7 | 6 | 8 | 7 | 6 | 5 | 6 | 5 | 4 |

The list contains all possible ways in which 12 can be written as the sum of 3 counting numbers. The lengths of the 3 sides, in inches, must be either 2, 5, and 5, 3, 4, and 5, or 4, 4, and 4. Why?

5–A.    Jill randomly tossed 3 darts at the board shown below. All hit the target. To win a prize, her total score must be either 66 or 75. Find all possible winning combinations.

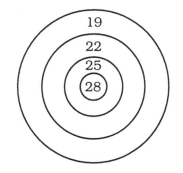

5–B.    Fred has a collection of dimes and quarters worth $2.50. Which of the following cannot be the total number of coins in his collection?

| 10 | 13 | 16 | 18 | 19 | 22 | 25 |
|----|----|----|----|----|----|----|
| 10 x25 | 5 D | 10 D | ✗ | 15 D | 20 D | 25 D |
| | 8 Q | 6 Q | | 4 Q | 2 Q | |

## MIXED STRATEGY PRACTICE

1. Guess and Test
2. Use a Variable
3. Draw a Picture
4. Look for a Pattern
5. Make a List

5-1.   1   1   2   3   5   8   13   21   ...

Use a pattern similar to the one shown above to help you fill in the missing numbers in each of the below sequences.

a.   1   2   __   __   __   __   21

b.   6   __   1   __   -3   __   -10

c.   2   __   __   0   __   __   2

d.   __   __   __   17   __   __   73

5-2. In how many ways can 3 girls divide 10 pennies if each must end up with at least one penny?

36

5-3. How many odd counting numbers less than 1,000 are not divisible by 7?

5-4. Each of three boxes X, Y, and Z contains at least 4 marbles. The total number of marbles is 36. There are twice as many marbles in box X as in box Y and box Z contains an odd number of marbles. What is the smallest number of marbles that could be in box Z?

Box Z   9  (X: 18  Y: 9)

## Solve a Simpler Problem

$3333333334^2$ equals a 20-digit number. What is the sum of the digits?

## SOLUTION

Problem:   $3333333334^2$ equals a  20-digit number.  What is the sum of the digits?

Solution:   Look at simpler related problems.

$$34^2 \qquad\qquad 334^2 \qquad\qquad 3334^2$$

$$1156 \qquad\quad 111556 \qquad\quad 11115556$$

Look for a pattern.

$$3333333334^2 = \underbrace{111...1}_{\text{Ten 1's}}\ \underbrace{555...5}_{\text{Nine 5's}}\,6$$

Sum of the digits:  $10 + 45 + 6 = \underline{\underline{61}}$

a.   Why was the Solve a Simpler Problem strategy used in this problem?
b.   The 3 and 4 involved in this problem are consecutive digits.  Will any similar problem with consecutive digits result in a pattern?

## DISCUSSION

The Solve a Simpler Problem strategy can be used in solving many complex problems by looking at simpler related cases.  A list of the data generated provides further insight and often reveals a pattern that suggests a solution.

## CLUES

The Solve a Simpler Problem strategy may be appropriate when:

*    The problem involves complicated computations.
*    The problem involves very large or very small numbers.
*    You are asked to find the sum of a series of numbers.
*    A direct solution is too complex.
*    You want to gain a better understanding of the problem.
*    The problem involves a large array or diagram.

## PRACTICE PROBLEMS

---

Problem:   In how many different ways can a dozen identical red chips be placed into three
           separate piles if each pile must end up with at least one chip?

Solution:   Solve a Simpler Problem

3 chips:      1  1  1   (1 way)    4 chips:   1  1  2    1  2  1    2  1  1   (3 ways)

Show that  5  chips can be put into the piles  6  ways.

| Number of chips | 3 | 4 | 5 | 6 | 7 | 8 | ... | 12 |
|---|---|---|---|---|---|---|---|---|
| Number of ways | 1 | 3 | 6 | 10 | 15 | 21 | | |

The pattern suggests that the answer to the problem is  55.  Verify.

---

6–A.   How many different rectangles are there in
       the figure shown at right?

6–B.   A box contains a set of  864  chips.  Each chip has either

one dot ( • ) , two dots ( •• ) , or no dots ( ) on one side.  Most of the
864  chips  have  one  dot  and  exactly  half  of  the  other  chips  have  2 dots.
What is the total number of dots on all 864 chips?

24

# MIXED STRATEGY PRACTICE

**PROBLEM-SOLVING STRATEGIES**

1. Guess and Test
2. Use a Variable
3. Draw a Picture
4. Look for a Pattern
5. Make a List
6. Solve a Simpler Problem

6–1. Thirteen identical rectangular cards are arranged as shown to form a large rectangle of perimeter 53 centimeters. What is the area of the large rectangle?

6–2. Find three perfect squares whose product is 45 less than the largest 4-digit perfect cube.

6–3. What is the average of the following pattern of numbers hidden under the cloud?

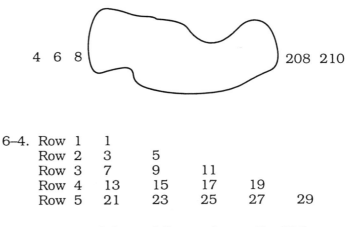

4  6  8                    208  210

6–4.

| | | | | |
|---|---|---|---|---|
| Row 1 | 1 | | | |
| Row 2 | 3 | 5 | | |
| Row 3 | 7 | 9 | 11 | |
| Row 4 | 13 | 15 | 17 | 19 |
| Row 5 | 21 | 23 | 25 | 27 | 29 |

a. Find the middle number in the 99th row.
b. What is the sum of the numbers in the 30th row?
c. Find the difference between the first number in row 90 and the first number in row 89.

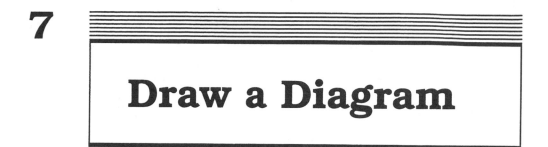

# Draw a Diagram

## Lake City Jr. High Students

* 12 out of every 18 ride a bus to school.
* 9 out of every 15 live in Lake City.
* 160 ride a bus to school.

**How many of the Jr. High students do not live in Lake City?**

## SOLUTION

Problem:   Lake City Jr. High Students

* 12 out of every 18 ride a bus to school.
* 9 out of every 15 live in Lake City.
* 160 ride a bus to school.

How many of the Jr. High students do not live in Lake City?

Solution:   Ride the bus:  12 out of 18, or 2 out of 3
Live in Lake City:  9 out of 15, or 3 out of 5

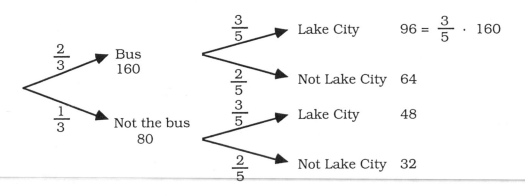

$96 = \dfrac{3}{5} \cdot 160$

96 students do not live in Lake City

a.  A tree diagram was used to help solve this problem.  Is a Venn diagram also useful in solving the problem?  Why or why not?
b.  The solution shows that 80 students do not ride the bus.  Explain why 48 of those students must live in Lake City.

## DISCUSSION

The Draw a Diagram strategy can often be used to systematically represent the details in a problem.  For example, the tree diagram to the right shows all 3-digit numbers less than 300 that contain only the digits 2, 3, 5, and 6 if each digit must be different.

$$2 \begin{cases} 3 \begin{cases} 5 \\ 6 \end{cases} \\ 5 \begin{cases} 3 \\ 6 \end{cases} \\ 6 \begin{cases} 3 \\ 5 \end{cases} \end{cases}$$

## CLUES

The Draw a Diagram strategy may be appropriate when:

* The problem involves sets, prime factorization, ratios, or probabilities.
* An actual picture can be drawn, but a diagram is more efficient.
* Representing relationships among quantities.

## PRACTICE PROBLEMS

Problem:   In a group of 37 people, 18 are neither overweight nor lawyers. Ten are overweight and 13 are lawyers. How many lawyers in the group are not overweight?

Solution:   Draw a Diagram

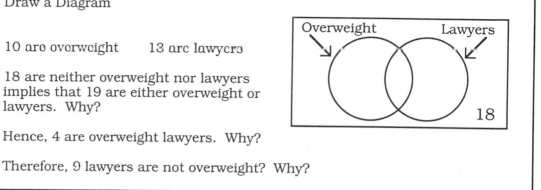

10 are overweight      13 are lawyers

18 are neither overweight nor lawyers implies that 19 are either overweight or lawyers. Why?

Hence, 4 are overweight lawyers. Why?

Therefore, 9 lawyers are not overweight? Why?

7–A.   If all of the digits must be different, how many 3-digit odd numbers greater than 700 can be written using only the digits 1, 2, 3, 5, 6, and 7?

7–B.   Of the 36 cars in a parking lot, 6 are red compact cars, 5 are red 2-door cars, and 7 are 2-door compacts. Half are not red, 13 are compacts, 20 have 4 doors, and 2 of the compact 4-door cars are not red. How many of the red 4-door cars in the parking lot are not compacts?

# MIXED STRATEGY PRACTICE

**PROBLEM-SOLVING STRATEGIES**

1. Guess and Test
2. Use a Variable
3. Draw a Picture
4. Look for a Pattern
5. Make a List
6. Solve a Simpler Problem
7. Draw a Diagram

7–1. Two men, each weighing 200 pounds, and their two sons weighing 100 pounds each, crossed a river in a small boat that can carry only 200 pounds. How did they manage to cross the river?

7–2. In how many different ways can Ted, Amy and Bart divide 9 nickels if each gets at least one nickel and each must end up with a different amount of money?

7–3. A computer company has 11 sales offices. Each office is to be connected to all the other offices by a direct telephone line. How many telephone lines will be needed to complete the job?

7–4. A scout troop took in $800 selling T-shirts and caps at the County Fair. They sold 200 T-shirts and 60 caps. How many youth T-shirts did they sell based on the following unit prices?

| | |
|---|---|
| Adult T's: | $4.00 |
| Youth T's: | $3.00 |
| Caps: | $2.00 |

# 8

# Use Direct Reasoning

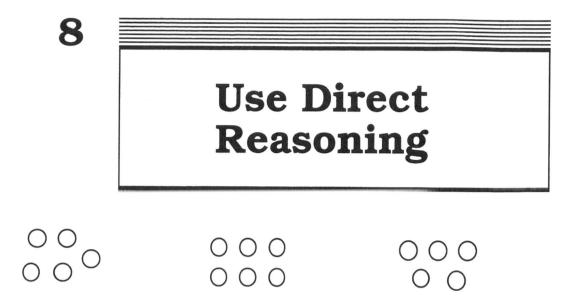

Each chip in two of the piles shown above weighs 8 grams. Each chip in the other pile weighs 7 grams. Show how to determine the pile that contains the 7-gram chips with only one weighing on a postal scale (not a balance scale).

## SOLUTION

Problem:

Each chip in two of the piles shown above weighs 8 grams.  Each chip in the other pile weighs 7 grams.  Show how to determine the pile that contains the 7-gram chips with only one weighing on a postal scale (not a balance scale).

Solution.  Take 1 chip from pile A, 2 from B, and 3 from C.

| | |
|---|---|
| Total weight = 47 g. | A  has the 7-gram chips |
| Total weight = 46 g. | B  has the 7-gram chips |
| Total weight = 45 g. | C  has the 7-gram chips |

a.  Are these the only possible total weights that may be obtained by choosing six chips in this manner?  Explain.
b.  Could this problem have been solved by placing all the chips on a scale?  Why or why not?

## DISCUSSION

Most problems involve the use of the Direct Reasoning strategy in conjunction with other strategies.  Problems where direct reasoning is useful are often of the form "If $A_1$, $A_2$, $A_3$,...., then B" where a conclusion B holds true when a series of one or more given conditions also hold true.  For example, the problem "If $x$, $y$, and $z$ are odd, then $x + 2y + 3z$ is even" is solved directly by first assuming that $x$, $y$, and $z$ are odd, and then observing that $x$ and $3z$ are odd and $2y$ is even.  Hence, $x + 2y + 3z$ must be even.

## CLUES

The Use Direct Reasoning Strategy may be appropriate when:

* A proof is required.
* A statement of the form "If ..., then..." is involved.
* You see a statement that you want to imply from a collection of known conditions.

## PRACTICE PROBLEMS

Problem:  There are 24 coins and a balance scale.  The coins are alike in every way except that one of them is counterfeit and slightly heavier than the other 23 coins. What is the least number of weighings needed on the balance scale to determine the heavier coin?

Solution:  Use Direct Reasoning

I                          II                          III

The figures shown above represent a solution to the problem.  Why?  Could the counterfeit coin be determined in 3 weighings when the total number of coins is 25?  26?  27?  28?

8–A.    Use the given clues to find the number represented by each letter.

* All are different one-digit whole numbers.
* The 4 corner numbers are all even.
* F is less than C and  C × F = 0.
* ABC is a 3–digit number divisible by 9.
* D is a prime number.
* A + D = 10  and  B + E = 13.
* E is one more than the average of A, B, and C.

A        B        C

D        E        F

8–B.    There are two boxes.  One contains $100 and the other contains one penny.  There are also two computers.  One always tells the truth about the boxes and the other one never tells the truth.  You don't know which box contains $100, nor which computer always tells the truth.  You are allowed to ask one question of one computer.  What question should you ask to be sure of selecting the box that contains $100?

# MIXED STRATEGY PRACTICE

8–1. Two baseball teams, A and B, played a double header. Use the clues given below to find all possible scores for the two games.

  * Team A won the 1st game by 3 runs.
  * Team B won the 2nd game by 1 run.
  * Team A scored a total of 11 runs.
  * Team B scored a total of 9 runs.

8–2. How many ways are there to get to the top of a ten step stairway if you take either one or two steps at a time?  89

8–3. After being warned about the dangers of smoking, a man decided to cut back 2 cigarettes a day. Keeping his promise, he continued cutting back 2 per day for one week. He smoked 91 cigarettes during the week. How many did he smoke the day before he started to cut back?

8–4. A computer was used to find the sum of the first 22 terms in the sequence of numbers whose first six terms are shown below. What digit is in the thousands place of the sum?

7, 77, 777, 7777, 77777, 777777, . . .

, . . 8624

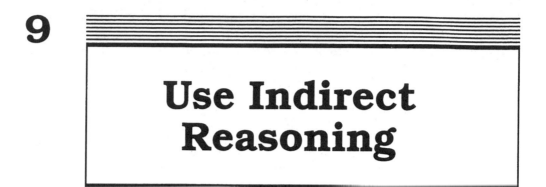

# 9

# Use Indirect Reasoning

Show how 2 nickels, 4 dimes, and 3 quarters can be placed into a 3 by 3 array so that each row and column contains a different amount of money.

## SOLUTION

Problem:   Show how 2 nickels, 4 dimes, and 3 quarters can be placed into a 3 by 3 array so that each row and column contains a different amount of money.

Solution:   First show why the coins in the 4 corners cannot all be dimes.

Suppose there is a dime in each corner.  Then  X, Y, Z, and W  must be coins of different denominations.  (Impossible.)  Why?  Therefore, the 4 coins in the corners cannot all be dimes.

Then show why the 3 quarters cannot all be in the same row or column.

| Q | Q | Q |
| W | X | D |
| Y | Z | D |

Suppose all the quarters are in the top row.  This means that there must be 2 dimes in the same column.  Why?  Two dimes and 2 nickels remain.  Hence, there is no solution.  Why?  Therefore, the 3 quarters cannot all be in the top row.

Solve the problem.

| D | Q | D | 45 |
| D | Q | Q | 60 |
| D | N | N | 20 |

30 55 40

a.   Does the discussion in the second part above guarantee that the 3 quarters cannot be in the same row or column?
b.   Why is Indirect Reasoning useful in solving this problem?

## DISCUSSION

The Use Indirect Reasoning strategy is helpful when a direct solution is either too complex or impossible.  For example, suppose you are asked to prove that every odd counting number that is a perfect square is the square of an odd number.  Looking directly at several examples such as  25,  49,  and  81  suggests that the statement is true.  However, this does not prove that it is always true.  In using indirect reasoning, we start by assuming that the number is even  $(2n)$,  after which it can easily be shown that its square, $4n^2$, is also even.  Hence, we can conclude that the number must be odd.

## CLUES

The Use Indirect Reasoning strategy may be appropriate when:

*   Direct Reasoning seems too complex or does not lead to a solution.
*   Assuming the negation of what you are trying to prove narrows the scope of the problem.
*   A proof is required.

## PRACTICE PROBLEMS

Problem:  Three burglars were caught breaking into a store.  When questioned by the police, at least one of the 3 told the truth and at least one of the 3 lied.  The statements made were as follows:

Bob:   It was Ken's idea.
Ken:   That's right, it was my idea.
Barb:  It wasn't my idea.

Show why it could not have been Barb's idea to rob the store.

Solution:  Use Indirect Reasoning

Suppose it was Barb's idea to rob the store.
Therefore, Bob lied.
We can now conclude that Ken lied.
This means that all three lied.  Why?
This is impossible since at least one of the three told the truth.
Hence, it was not Barb's idea.

9–A.    Five consecutive whole numbers whose sum is odd satisfy the following condition: $A + C + E = B + C + D$. Show why C cannot be even.

9–B.    Suppose you know that one of the statements on the cards represented below is true and the other is false.  Show why the triangle cannot be on the back side of card A.

| This card has a triangle drawn on the back side and the other card has a circle on the back | One of these cards has a triangle drawn on the back side and one of the cards has a circle on the back. |

Card A                                                        Card B

# MIXED STRATEGY PRACTICE

1. Guess and Test
2. Use a Variable
3. Draw a Picture
4. Look for a Pattern
5. Make a List
6. Solve a Simpler Problem
7. Draw a Diagram
8. Use Direct Reasoning
9. Use Indirect Reasoning

9–1. A farmer constructed a fence around a square field which is 400 meters on each side. He then divided the field into four equal areas by constructing fences across the middle vertically and horizontally. If all of the posts in the fence are 8 meters apart, how many posts did he use?

9–2. What is the remainder when $5^{99}$ is divided by:

   a.   2?          b.   3?          c.   7?

9–3. Kennedy won the city track meet with 84 points. Lincoln scored twice as many points as Jefferson and Madison scored half as many points as Jefferson. Altogether, the total for two of the four teams was 95 and the total number of points scored by all teams was greater than 200. How many points did Lincoln score in the track meet?

9–4. During my vacation last summer it rained on 13 days. But when it rained in the morning, the afternoon was dry. Also, every rainy afternoon was preceded by a dry morning. There were 11 dry mornings and 12 dry afternoons. How many days long was my vacation?

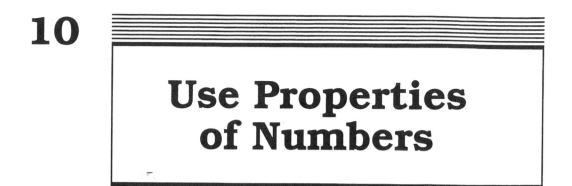

# 10

# Use Properties of Numbers

The owner of the Pizza Palace purchased 3 dozen caps for the softball teams he sponsors. He wanted to keep the price below $10 per cap. If one of the following represents the total cost, what was the cost per cap? Here, A, B, and C represent the hundreds digits.

$A06.40        $B51.24        $C39.68

you lika de hats?

## SOLUTION

Problem:  The owner of the Pizza Palace purchased 3 dozen caps for the softball teams he
sponsors.  He wanted to keep the price below $10 per cap.  If one of the following
represents the total cost, what was the cost per cap?  Here, A, B, and C represent the hundreds digits.

$A06.40                      $B51.24                      $C39.68

Solution:  The total cost must be divisible by 4 and 9.  Why?
All given totals are divisible by 4.  Why?

9  divides  $A06.40  only when  A = 8
9  divides  $B51.24  only when  B = 6
9  divides  $C39.68  only when  C = 1

$806.40 ÷ 36 = $22.40      $139.68 ÷ 36 = $3.88      $651.24 ÷ 36 = $18.09

Thus, the cost for each cap was  $3.88.

a.  Why is there only one possible value for each of A, B, and C?
b.  Would Guess and Test be an efficient way to solve the problem?

## DISCUSSION

An understanding of properties of numbers often provides a more efficient way to solve a
problem involving whole numbers.  For example, knowing the divisibility tests for 4 and 9
allows one to quickly conclude that the number 4,000,000,032 is divisible by 36 even
though you might not be able to do this problem on your calculator.

## CLUES

The Use Properties of Numbers strategy may be appropriate when:

*   Special types of numbers such as odds, evens, primes, etc. are involved.
*   A problem can be simplified by using certain properties.
*   A problem involves lots of computation.

## PRACTICE PROBLEMS

Problem: Show why the numbers $M$ and $N$ shown below cannot be prime.

$M = 19^7 + 7^{19} \times (13^7 - 7^{13}) + 3^5$

$N = 17! + 253$ (Note: $17! = 17 \times 16 \times 15 \times \cdots \times 3 \times 2 \times 1$)

Solution: Use Properties of Numbers

$19^7, 7^{19}, 13^7, 7^{13}$, and $3^5$ must all be odd numbers. Why?
M = odd + odd × even + odd = even. Why?
Hence, M cannot be a prime number. Why?

17! and 253 are both divisible by 11. Why?
Therefore, 11 divides N = (17! + 253).
Hence, N cannot be a prime number.

10–A. Find my 3-digit house number with the help of the following clues.

* If you add 1 to the number, it is a multiple of 8.
* If you add 5 to the number, it is a multiple of 9.
* If you add 2 to the number, it is a multiple of 11.

10–B. I am a 4-digit number with no repeating digits. I am divisible by 5, my first two digits (left to right) make a number divisible by 3, and my first three digits make a number divisible by 4. Also, my digits have a sum of 19 and I have the digit 7 in the thousands place. Who am I?

# MIXED STRATEGY PRACTICE

**PROBLEM-SOLVING STRATEGIES**

1. Guess and Test
2. Use a Variable
3. Draw a Picture
4. Look for a Pattern
5. Make a List
6. Solve a Simpler Problem
7. Draw a Diagram
8. Use Direct Reasoning
9. Use Indirect Reasoning
10. Use Properties of Numbers

10–1. Jim decided to put his collection of rare coins into a set of cups that are lined up on the kitchen table. Trying to put 5 coins into each cup, he ended up with only 2 coins in the last cup. When he put 3 coins into each cup, he had 9 coins left over. There are less than ten cups on the table. How many rare coins does Jim have?

10–2. How many different triangles are there in the given figure?

10–3. Karen and Beth bought identical boxes of stationery. Beth used hers to write one sheet letters and Karen used hers to write two sheet letters. Beth used all her envelopes and had 16 sheets left over. Karen used all her sheets and had 7 envelopes left over. How many envelopes were there in each box?

10–4. Mr. Leung builds ring-toss games with 1, 3 or 4 pegs. One day, he used 51 pegs to build 20 games. Find at least two different ways in which this can be done.

# 11

## Solve an Equivalent Problem

At Tommie's yogurt shop you can order either a plain vanilla yogurt or you can order it with one or more of 6 toppings. How many different types of yogurt dishes can be ordered?

## SOLUTION

Problem:   At Tommie's yogurt shop you can order either a plain vanilla yogurt or you can order it with one or more of 6 toppings.  How many different types of yogurt dishes can be ordered?

Solution:   An equivalent problem is to determine the number of sets that are subsets of the 6–element set {A, B, C, D, E, F}.  Why? The empty set represents a plain yogurt. By looking at simpler cases we can easily show that {A} has 2 subsets, {A, B} has 4 subsets, and {A, B, C} has 8 subsets.  Extending this pattern suggests that the set {A, B, C, D, E, F} has 64 subsets.  Hence, there are 64 ways to order a yogurt at Tommie's Yogurt Shop

a.  How many ways can a yogurt with exactly 2 toppings be ordered at Tommie's Yogurt Shop?
b.  How many ways can a yogurt with up to $n$ toppings be ordered at Tommie's Yogurt Shop?

## DISCUSSION

The Solve an Equivalent Problem strategy is helpful when you can recall a similar problem previously solved or when you can find an equivalent problem that is easier to solve.  For example, in trying to find the number of terms in the sequence  4, 11, 18, 25, ..., 487, you could look at the  corresponding sequence 7, 14, 21, 28, ..., 490  and more easily conclude that there are 70 terms.

## CLUES

The Solve an Equivalent Problem strategy may be appropriate when:

* You can find an equivalent problem that is easier to solve.
* A problem is related to another problem you have previously solved.
* A problem can be represented in a more familiar setting.
* A geometric problem can be represented algebraically or vice versa.
* Physical problems can be easily represented with numbers or symbols.

## PRACTICE PROBLEMS

| | |
|---|---|
| Problem: | What is the 100th term in the sequence shown below? |
| | 13     20     27     34     41     . . . |
| Solution: | Solve an Equivalent Problem |
| | One way to solve this problem is to look at a similar sequence. |

| | | | | | |
|---|---|---|---|---|---|
| Given sequence: | 13 | 20 | 27 | 34 | . . . |
| Similar sequence: | 14 | 21 | 28 | 35 | . . . |
| Another sequence: | 7 | 14 | 21 | 28 | . . . |

It is easy to show that the 100th term in the last sequence is 700. Why? Thus, the 100th term in the given sequence is 706.

11–A.  In how many different ways could five players of the girls' basketball team be paired up to dance with five players on the boys' basketball team?

11–B.  In how many ways can a committee of two be selected from a group of eight girls?

# MIXED STRATEGY PRACTICE

PROBLEM-SOLVING
STRATEGIES

1. Guess and Test
2. Use a Variable
3. Draw a Picture
4. Look for a Pattern
5. Make a List
6. Solve a Simpler Problem
7. Draw a Diagram
8. Use Direct Reasoning
9. Use Indirect Reasoning
10. Use Properties of Numbers
11. Solve an Equivalent Problem

11-1. I am thinking of 3 different counting numbers. The smallest number is 2 less than half the largest, the average of the 3 numbers is 13, and one of the numbers is a 2-digit prime. What are the numbers?

11-2. If it takes 5 cans of dog food to feed 4 dogs for one day, how many dogs can you feed for 4 days with 40 cans of dog food?

11-3. All but five of my pets are cats.
All but five of my pets are rabbits.
All but four of my pets are dogs.
I have only cats, rabbits, and dogs.
How many pets do I have? What are they?

11-4. Three chips are hidden under 3 cups labeled X, Y, and Z.

Randy and Linda both know that the hidden chips were selected from a set of 2 blue and 3 red chips. After being shown only the chips under cups Y and Z, Randy was asked "What color is the chip under cup X?" He replied, "I can't tell for sure." Knowing Randy's reply, Linda was then shown the chips under cups X and Z. When asked for the color of the chip under cup Y, she said, "I can't tell for sure." Explain why the chip under cup Z must be red.

# 12

## Work Backward

Kay and Jim are playing a game in which they take turns removing either one or two chips from a pile of chips. The person who removes the last chip loses the game. Suppose it is Kay's turn and there are 17 chips left. Find a strategy that will make her a sure winner.

## SOLUTION

Problem:   Kay and Jim are playing a game in which they take turns removing either one or two chips from a pile of chips. The person who removes the last chip loses the game. Suppose it is Kay's turn and there are 17 chips left. Find a strategy that will make her a sure winner.

Solution:   We start by looking at the end of the game. If it is Jim's turn when only one chip is left, he will have to remove the last chip and lose the game. Working back, suppose there are 4 chips left and it is Jim's turn. If he takes one chip, Kay should then take 2; if he takes 2 chips, Kay should take one. In either case, Jim must take the last chip making Kay the winner. Continuing to work backward, it can be shown that if there are 7, 10, 13, or 16 chips left when it is Jim's turn, Kay can be a sure winner.

a.   What is it about this problem that suggests the Work Backward strategy?
b.   In playing this game, would you want to be the first player if there are 28 chips at the start ?  Why or why not?
c.   Can the first player always win?  Explain.
d.   Suppose the rules are changed so that the player removing the last chip is the winner. Find a winning strategy.

## DISCUSSION

Some problems are more easily solved by working backward from the end result to the initial condition. For example, consider this problem: How much money did Adam have to start with if he ended up with $6.25 after spending $3.00 more than half his savings to buy a shirt? By working backward from $6.25 it is easily seen that he spent $9.25. But this is half his savings. Thus, he started with $18.50.

## CLUES

The Work Backward strategy may be appropriate when:

*   The final result is clear and the initial portion of a problem is obscure.
*   A problem proceeds from being complex initially to being simple at the end.
*   A direct approach involves a complicated equation.
*   A problem involves a sequence of reversible actions.

**PRACTICE PROBLEMS** ≡≡≡≡≡≡≡≡≡≡≡≡≡≡≡≡≡≡≡≡≡≡≡≡≡≡

Problem:  Helen paid 25 cents for a bag of jellybeans. After giving her brother half the beans, she ate 13. Her sister then ate one more than half the remaining beans, after which there were 3 left. How many jellybeans were in the bag before it was opened?

Solution:  Work Backward

End                                                  Start

| 3 | → | | → | | → | ? |

| 3 | →(3+1)2→ | 8 | →8+13→ | 21 | →2 × 21→ | 42 |

The figure above represents a solution to the problem. Try to explain each step as you work backward from the end result.

12–A.  Two cans X and Y both contain some water. From X Tim pours as much water into Y as Y already contains. Then from Y he pours as much water into X as X presently has. Finally, he pours from X into Y as much water as Y presently has. Each can now contains 24 ounces of water. How many ounces of water were in each can at the start?

12–B.  Karen spent all but $8.00 of her savings in three stores. In each store she spent $2.00 less than half of what she had when she went in. How much money did Karen have at the start?

# MIXED STRATEGY PRACTICE

**PROBLEM-SOLVING STRATEGIES**

1. Guess and Test
2. Use a Variable
3. Draw a Picture
4. Look for a Pattern
5. Make a List
6. Solve a Simpler Problem
7. Draw a Diagram
8. Use Direct Reasoning
9. Use Indirect Reasoning
10. Use Properties of Numbers
11. Solve an Equivalent Problem
12. Work Backward

12-1. Four teams (A, B, C, D) in the all-star basketball league played each other at home and away. Use the clues below to find the won/lost record for each team.

A won all of its home games.
D never defeated C.
C won 3 games, one of which was at home.
B won 4 games.
D lost all its home games.

12-2. A group of girls is standing equally spaced around a circle. The 43rd girl is directly opposite the 89th girl. How many girls are there?

12-3. In a group of 60 middle school students, 26 are boys, 26 are in grade eight, and 15 are neither 7th nor 8th graders. Of the girls, 9 are in grade seven, and 12 are in grade eight. How many boys in the group are in the seventh grade?

12-4. Use the number line shown below to help you find the number between $x$ and $y$ that is twice as far from 3/8 as half of 5/6 is from 2/3.

```
      X                                          Y
 ──o──o────o──────────o────o────o──────────o──
   0   3/8          2/3  5/6   1
```

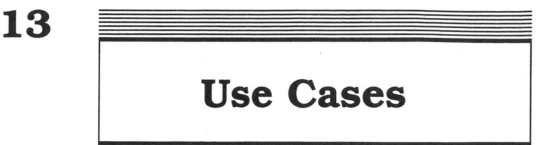

# 13

# Use Cases

A 23 member university committee consists of freshmen, sophomores, juniors, seniors, and graduate students. Each class is represented by a different number of students and each has at least one student on the committee. The freshmen and seniors total 9, the sophomores and seniors total 13, and the senior and graduate students total 8. Find the number of committee members from each class if one of the classes is represented by 5 students.

# SOLUTION

Problem:   A 23 member university committee consists of freshmen, sophomores, juniors, seniors, and graduate students.  Each class is represented by a different number of students and each has at least one student on the committee.  The freshmen and seniors total 9, the sophomores and seniors total 13, and the senior and graduate students total 8.  Find the number of committee members from each class if one of the classes is represented by 5 students.

Solution:   Since one of the classes is represented by 5 students, we can solve this problem by looking  at several cases.  Suppose there are 5 freshmen on the committee. This means that there will be 4 seniors and 1 graduate students.  The case with 5 graduate students on the committee means that there would be 3 seniors, 6 freshmen, and 10 sophomores.  Explain why neither of these cases leads to a solution.  Continuing in this way, it can be shown that the committee consists of 3 freshmen, 7 sophomores, 5 juniors, 6 seniors, and 2 graduate students.

a.   What is it about this problem that suggests the Use Cases strategy?
b.   Show why there cannot be exactly 5 sophomores or exactly 5 seniors on the committee.
c.   Show why there cannot be 5 juniors and 7 seniors on the committee.

# DISCUSSION

Problems can often be solved by considering various cases.  For example, in trying to find the numbers for which the inequality $(x + 2)(x - 1) > 0$ is true, we need only consider the cases where $(x + 2)$ and $(x - 1)$ are both positive or both negative. If $(x + 2) > 0$ and $(x - 1) > 0$, then $x > 1$. If $(x + 2) < 0$ and $(x - 1) < 0$, then $x < -2$. Therefore, $(x + 2)(x - 1) > 0$ when $x > 1$ or $x < -2$.

# CLUES

The Use Cases strategy may be appropriate when:

*   A problem can be separated into several distinct cases.
*   A problem involves distinct collections of numbers like odds and evens, primes and composite,  positives and negatives, etc.
*   Investigations in specific cases can be generalized.

## PRACTICE PROBLEMS

---

**Problem:** If $x$ and $y$ are integers, when will $x^2 + xy + (x - y)$ be odd?

**Solution:** Use Cases

| | $x$ | $y$ | $x^2$ | $xy$ | $x - y$ | $x^2 + xy + (x - y)$ |
|---|---|---|---|---|---|---|
| Case 1 | odd | odd | odd | odd | even | even |
| Case 2 | odd | even | odd | even | odd | even |
| Case 3 | even | odd | even | even | odd | odd |
| Case 4 | even | even | even | even | even | even |

Hence, $x^2 + xy + (x - y)$ is odd when $x$ is even and $y$ is odd.

---

13–A.  A hexomino consists of 6 congruent squares joined at complete sides.  For example,

is a hexomino but          is not.

Find all the hexominoes that have exactly 4 squares in a line.

13–B.  Cody has a collection of baseball cards.  Is it possible for him to place the cards into 5 boxes so that  exactly 3 of the boxes contain an odd number of cards and the total number of cards in two of the boxes is the same as the total number in the other 3 boxes? Explain.

# MIXED STRATEGY PRACTICE

**PROBLEM-SOLVING STRATEGIES**

1. Guess and Test
2. Use a Variable
3. Draw a Picture
4. Look for a Pattern
5. Make a List
6. Solve a Simpler Problem
7. Draw a Diagram
8. Use Direct Reasoning
9. Use Indirect Reasoning
10. Use Properties of Numbers
11. Solve an Equivalent Problem
12. Work Backward
13. Use Cases

13-1. A sport shop is having a "30% off" sale on tennis balls and racquet balls. Tennis balls are sold in cans of 3 balls and racquet balls are sold in cans of 2 balls. One customer bought 49 balls. How many tennis balls did she buy if she left the store with 19 cans?

13-2. How many children are there in a family where each girl has as many brothers as sisters, but each boy has twice as many sisters as brothers?

13-3. After previewing the pairings for the first round of the state basketball single elimination tournament, each of three sportswriters chose the teams that they thought would win in the first round. Fridley was the only team not picked to win by any of the writers. The predictions were as follows:

Sportswriter #1: Duluth, Cambridge, Alexandria, St. Cloud
Sportswriter #2: Edina, Alexandria, Mankato, Cambridge
Sportswriter #3: St. Cloud, Mankato, Alexandria, Hopkins

Find the pairings for the first round of the tournament.

13-4. There are 2 piles with 4 chips in each pile. Two players take turns removing either one chip from one of the piles or one chip from each of the 2 piles. The winner is the player that removes the last chip. Find a winning strategy for this game.

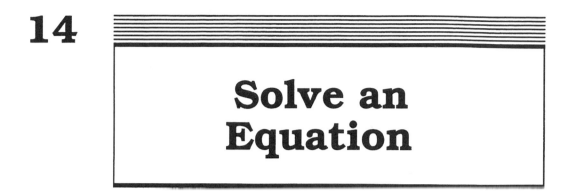

# 14

# Solve an Equation

A marching band needs to raise $13,500 for a trip to the Rose Bowl. The director told the band members that one-third of the amount that has been raised so far is equal to half of the amount that is still needed. How much more money needs to be raised for the trip?

## SOLUTION

**Problem:**   A marching band needs to raise $13,500 for a trip to the Rose Bowl.  The director told the band members that one-third of the amount that has been raised so far is equal to half of the amount that is still needed.  How much more money needs to be raised for the trip?

**Solution:**   Let $x$ = the amount of money that still needs to be raised.  Thus, the amount raised so far is  $13,500 - x$ .  Hence we have

$$\frac{1}{2}x = \frac{1}{3}(13,500 - x)$$
$$3x = 2(13,500 - x)$$
$$3x = 27,000 - 2x$$
$$5x = 27,000$$
$$x = 5,400$$

Therefore, $5,400 still needs to be raised.

a.  Why does $13,500 - x$ represent the amount of money that has been raised so far?
b.  What equation results if we start by letting $y$ equal the amount of money raised so far?
c.  Explain why Guess and Test is not an appropriate strategy in solving this problem.

## DISCUSSION

Many problems can best be solved by introducing a variable and then representing the given information with an equation.  For example, consider the following problem:

What is Andrew's weight if he weighs 44 pounds plus half his weight?

If $n$ is Andrew's weight, then the problem suggests the equation $n = 44 + \frac{n}{2}$ .
Solving for $n$ yields that Andrew weighs 88 pounds.

## CLUES

The Solve an Equation  strategy may be appropriate when:

*    A variable has been introduced.
*    The words "is", "is equal to",  or "equals"  appear in a problem.
*    The stated conditions can easily be represented with an equation.

## PRACTICE PROBLEMS

| | |
|---|---|
| Problem: | Find three pairs of nonzero numbers $x$ and $y$ where one-half their sums equals twice their product. |

Solution:    Solve an Equation

Half the sum = twice the product     $\frac{1}{2}(x+y) = 2xy$

Therefore, $y = \dfrac{x}{(4x-1)}$.      Verify.

Let $x = 1$. Then $y = \frac{1}{3}$.   Check: $\frac{1}{2}\left(1 + \frac{1}{3}\right) = \frac{2}{3} = 2(1)\left(\frac{1}{3}\right)$

Let $x = 2$. Then $y = \frac{2}{7}$.   Check: $\frac{1}{2}\left(2 + \frac{2}{7}\right) = \frac{8}{7} = 2(2)\left(\frac{2}{7}\right)$

An infinite number of pairs $(x, y)$ satisfy the conditions.

14–A.   Traveling at a certain speed, it took Mark 5 hours to drive from his home to Denver. If he had driven 2 miles per hour faster, he would have arrived in Denver 12 minutes earlier. How far is it from Mark's home to Denver?   $d = 240$

14–B.   Katie: "Think of a number. Add 6. Multiply by 5. Subtract 28. Double it. Add 16. Multiply by 5. Subtract 50. Double it. Now tell me your result."

Jeff:   "900."

Katie quickly found the original number selected by Jeff. Explain her method.

# MIXED STRATEGY PRACTICE

**PROBLEM-SOLVING STRATEGIES**

1. Guess and Test
2. Use a Variable
3. Draw a Picture
4. Look for a Pattern
5. Make a List
6. Solve a Simpler Problem
7. Draw a Diagram
8. Use Direct Reasoning
9. Use Indirect Reasoning
10. Use Properties of Numbers
11. Solve an Equivalent Problem
12. Work Backward
13. Use Cases
14. Solve an Equation

14–1. Complete the following sequence so that, after the first two terms, each successive term is the average of all the preceding terms.

20 _____ _____ 28 _____ _____

14–2. There are 200 chips in a box. Some are red, some are white, and some are blue. Each chip is marked with either an odd number or an even number. There are 23 red–even chips, 14 blue–odd chips, 140 even chips, and 42 of the 72 white chips are white–even. How many chips in the box are red–odd? 16 How many chips in the box are blue–even? 15 *make a list*

14–3. Jane saved one quarter in March of 1984. Each month after that she saved 2 more quarters than she had saved the month before. If Jane continued saving quarters in this way, how much money, in dollars, would she have had at the end of February, 1989?

14–4. The Kennedy Pep Club rented a bus to take all of its members to a baseball game. The cost per person was to be $18.00. However, those making the trip had to pay $24.00 each because 10 members cancelled out at the last minute. How many pep club members took the bus to the game? 30 *Use a var.*

# 15

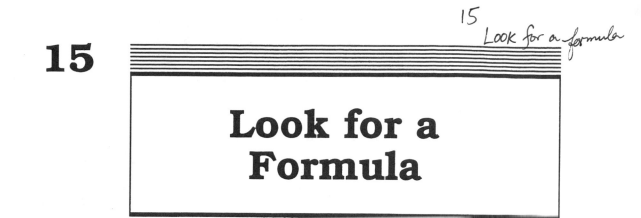

## Look for a Formula

A certain ball is dropped from an altitude of 1 meter and rebounds one–half of its previous altitude. What is the total distance the ball has traveled when it hits the floor the 40th time?

## SOLUTION

Problem:   A certain ball is dropped from an altitude of 1 meter and rebounds one–half of
           its previous altitude.  What is the total distance the ball has traveled when it hits
           the floor the 40th time?

Solution:   Consider the following representation:

| H = Hit Number | 1 | 2 | 3 | 4 | 5 | ... | 40 |
|---|---|---|---|---|---|---|---|
| T = Total Distance | 1 | 2 | $2\frac{1}{2}$ | $2\frac{3}{4}$ | $2\frac{7}{8}$ | ... | ? |

The pattern suggests that   $T = 2 + \dfrac{2^{38} - 1}{2^{38}}$   when  H = 40.

a.  Write the general term that represents the total distance the ball has traveled when it
    hits the floor the *n*th time.
b.  Will the total distance traveled by the ball ever be 3 meters?  Explain.

## DISCUSSION

Problems can often be solved by directly applying a formula with which we are familiar.  For
example, in trying to determine how long it will take to drive 450 miles while averaging  60
mph, we can use the formula  $d = rt$  ($d$ = distance, $r$ = rate, $t$ = time)  to show that it takes
7.5 hours.   There are also many situations where we must look for a "new" formula.
Problems of this type often involve a number pattern.  For example, when asked to find the
60th  term in the sequence  2, 5, 8, 11, 14, ...  we can conclude that it is 179 since the
formula for the *n*th  term is  $3n - 1$.

## CLUES

The Look for a Formula  strategy may be appropriate when:

*   A problem suggests a pattern that can be generalized.
*   Ideas such as percent, rate, distance, area, volume, or other measurable attributes are
    involved.
*   Applications in science, business, etc. are involved.
*   Solving problems involving topics like statistics, probability, etc.

## PRACTICE PROBLEMS

Problem: What is the $n$th term in the sequence shown below when $n$ is an even number?

$$\frac{1}{4} \quad \frac{1}{2} \quad \frac{1}{16} \quad \frac{1}{8} \quad \frac{1}{64} \quad \frac{1}{32} \quad \cdots$$

Solution: Look for a Formula

Note that the denominators are all powers of 2 and every numerator is 1.

| Term number: | 1 | 2 | 3 | 4 | 5 | 6 | |
|---|---|---|---|---|---|---|---|
| Denominator: | $4 = 2^2$ | $2 = 2^1$ | $16 = 2^4$ | $8 = 2^3$ | $64 = 2^6$ | $32 = 2^5$ | $\cdots$ |

The pattern suggests that the $n$th term is $\left(\frac{1}{2}\right)^{n-1}$ when $n$ is even. Why?

15–A. Find the 99th term in each sequence shown below.

a.    3     7     11     15     19     ...    *4n–1*

b.    8     16     32     64     128     ...    *$2^{n+2}$*

c.    2     6     12     20     30     ...    *n(n+1)*

15–B. A bottle contains one gallon of water. At 6 A.M. half the water is removed. At 7 A.M. half of the remaining water is removed. If this process of removing half the remaining water each hour continues, how much water will remain in the bottle at 11:30 A.M. the next day?    *$\frac{1}{2^{30}}$*

# MIXED STRATEGY PRACTICE

15–1. Find the sum of the 77 consecutive counting numbers whose first and last terms add up to 108.

15–2. Five percent of the students enrolled at a university were asked the question "Do you like math?" Of those surveyed, 1/3 were freshmen, 1/5 were sophomores, 1/6 were juniors, 1/4 were seniors, and 42 were graduate students. How many students are enrolled at the university?

15–3. Suppose a train traveling 90 miles per hour takes four seconds to enter a tunnel. From there it takes one minute before the train is completely outside the tunnel. Find the length of both the train and the tunnel.

15–4. A snail is at the bottom of a barrel and wants to climb out. It climbs half–way up the side of the barrel during the first hour, 1/3 of the remaining distance the second hour, 1/4 of the remaining distance the third, 1/5 of the remaining distance the fourth hour, and so on. If the snail continues in this way, how far from the top of the 96 centimeter high barrel will it be after 23 hours?

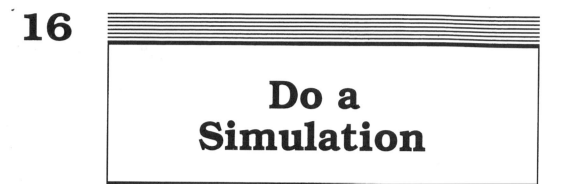

# 16

# Do a Simulation

The Cardinal baseball team is batting in the bottom of the ninth inning. The bases are loaded, there are 2 out, the score is tied, and Casey is at bat. Coach Robinson calls time out and tells Casey not to swing at any of the pitches since he knows that the pitcher throws strikes only 40% of the time. Conduct a simulation that will help you form an opinion about Coach Robinson's decision.

## SOLUTION

Problem:  The Cardinal baseball team is batting in the bottom of the ninth inning.  The bases are loaded, there are 2 out, the score is tied, and Casey is at bat.  Coach Robinson calls time out and tells Casey not to swing at any of the pitches since he knows that the pitcher throws strikes only 40% of the time.  Conduct a simulation that will help you form an opinion about Coach Robinson's decision.

Solution:  A random number table is one device that can be used to simulate this problem.  Let the one–digit numbers 0, 1, 2, and 3 represent a strike and let each of the other digits represent a ball.  One trial consists of reading the digits until you get either 3 strikes or 4 balls.  Three strikes means that the game will go into extra innings.  Four balls means that the Cardinals will win the game.  For example, consider the random digits shown below.

```
0 1 9 0 | 7 7 2 1 4 6 | 0 5 7 6 4 | 2 2 4 0 | 0 2 7 4 1
S S B S | B B S S B B | S B B B B | S S B S | S S B B S
            WIN            WIN
```

a.  Why is this assignment of digits representing strikes and balls appropriate?
b.  Describe an experiment that will simulate the problem by using a spinner or by using colored chips.
c.  Could a random number table have been used as a model for a pitcher that throws strikes 45% of the time?  If so, describe a method.  If not, why not?

## DISCUSSION

Problems that are too difficult to be analyzed theoretically can sometimes be simulated by repeatedly performing an experiment yielding data which can be used to estimate an answer.  Materials used in doing a simulation may consist of random number tables, dice, colored chips, slips of paper, coins, a calculator with a random number generator, or a computer.  For example, an experiment that involves many tosses of 5 coins where the number of heads (girls) and the number of tails (boys) are recorded can be used to estimate the probability that a family of 5 children consists of more girls than boys.

## CLUES

The Do a Simulation  strategy may be appropriate when:

*   A problem involves a complicated probability experiment.
*   An actual experiment is too difficult or impossible to perform.
*   A problem has a repeatable process that can be done experimentally.
*   Finding the actual answer requires techniques not previously developed.

### PRACTICE PROBLEMS

Problem:   Suppose a certain brand of frozen pizza has a prize in 30% of the packages. Conduct a simulation to estimate the average number of pizzas that must be purchased to win a prize.

Solution:   Do a Simulation

The problem can be simulated by using a spinner. Make a spinner where a sector of the circle comprises 30% of the circle. Spin the spinner repeatedly and record the number of times it takes until you first fall into the 30% sector. Repeat the experiment 50 times. The average number of times it takes to fall into the 30% sector for the 50 trials estimates the expected number of pizzas you will have to buy in order to win a prize.

16–A.  A game at a school carnival consists of 3 boxes (H, T, X) that contain either black or white chips as shown. A coin is tossed. If it is a head, a chip is randomly selected from box H and placed into box X. If it is a tail, a chip is randomly selected from box T and placed into box X. Then a chip is randomly selected from box X. To win a prize, the chip drawn from X must be white. Estimate the probability of winning a prize.

H         T         X

16–B.  A mouse is placed in box X of the maze shown below. There is a mouse trap in box Y. What is the probability that the mouse will be trapped if it randomly moves either left, right, or up throughout the maze ?

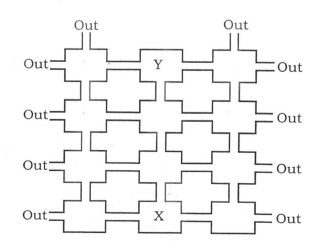

64

# MIXED STRATEGY PRACTICE

**PROBLEM-SOLVING STRATEGIES**

1. Guess and Test
2. Use a Variable
3. Draw a Picture
4. Look for a Pattern
5. Make a List
6. Solve a Simpler Problem
7. Draw a Diagram
8. Use Direct Reasoning
9. Use Indirect Reasoning
10. Use Properties of Numbers
11. Solve an Equivalent Problem
12. Work Backward
13. Use Cases
14. Solve an Equation
15. Look for a Formula
16. Do a Simulation

16-1. How many 5-digit numbers are divisible by 50?

16-2. A married couple wants to have 3 or 4 children and they want exactly 2 girls. Is it more likely that they will have exactly two girls with three children or exactly two with four children? 3\8

16-3. Use the clues below to find the number represented by each letter.

* All are 1-digit even natural numbers.
* A + B + C = 14.
* The one perfect square is in the top row.
* A = F and D = E.
* The sum of C and F is 12.
* The sum of D, E, and F is not 20.
* The number before the only 4 is the only prime.

A 8    B 2    C 4

D 8    E 8    F 8

16-4. Thirty percent of the chickens escaped from a maximum security coop. After a long search, 2/3 of the escapees were recaptured and returned to the coop. The number of chickens now in the coop is 216. How many were there before the great escape?

# 17

# Use a Model

All patterns shown below were formed by cutting along 4 edges of an open top cubical box. Label the square that was the bottom of the box and then determine how many side and/or bottom edges were cut to get the pattern. Two are done for you.

4 side edges

2 side edges
2 bottom edges

# SOLUTION

Problem:  All patterns shown below were formed by cutting along 4 edges of an open top cubical box.  Label the square that was the bottom of the box and then determine how many side and/or bottom edges were cut to get the pattern.  Two are done for you.

4  side edges

2  side edges
2 bottom edges

Solution:  Cut out the patterns and fold them into cubes to verify that the bases are labeled correctly.

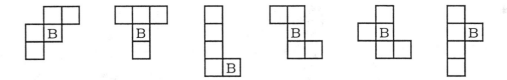

a.  Explain why the following patterns were not included in the figures shown above.

b.  What is a possible extension of this problem?

# DISCUSSION

The Use a Model strategy is helpful when a concrete representation using physical objects (e.g. wooden blocks or paper geometric shapes)  makes it easier to visualize the ideas involved in the problem.  For example, show how the shapes shown below can be arranged to form a square.

It is difficult to visualize the possible arrangements without actually having 5 paper or plastic pieces that can easily be rearranged physically.

# CLUES

The Use a Model  strategy may be appropriate when:

*   Physical objects can be used to represent the ideas involved.
*   A drawing is either too complex or inadequate to provide insight into the problem.
*   A problem involves 3–dimensional objects.

## PRACTICE PROBLEMS

| | |
|---|---|
| Problem: | Show how a 12 × 12 × 12 inch cube can be cut into 36 smaller cubes if the lengths of the edges of the smaller cubes must all be whole numbers. |

Solution:  Use a Model

Cut two 3 inch layers off the top of the cube.
Each of these pieces can then be cut into 16
smaller 3 × 3 inch cubes.
The remaining piece is 6 × 12 × 12 inches.
This piece can be cut into 4 cubes that
are each 6 × 6 × 6 inches.

This gives us 36 smaller cubes. (16 + 16 + 4 = 36)

17–A.   How many different surface areas are possible when 8 one inch cubes are arranged so that each has one or more faces in common (touching) with at least one of the other cubes?

17–B.   The square in Figure I was cut into 4 pieces as shown and then the pieces were arranged to form Figure II. Clearly, the square has area 16 × 16 or 256 square units. Notice that Figure II appears to be a rectangle with area 10 × 26 or 260 square units. Try to explain why these areas are different.

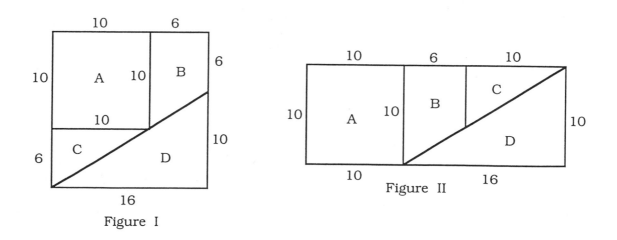

Figure I                              Figure II

68

# MIXED STRATEGY PRACTICE

**PROBLEM-SOLVING STRATEGIES**

1. Guess and Test
2. Use a Variable
3. Draw a Picture
4. Look for a Pattern
5. Make a List
6. Solve a Simpler Problem
7. Draw a Diagram
8. Use Direct Reasoning
9. Use Indirect Reasoning
10. Use Properties of Numbers
11. Solve an Equivalent Problem
12. Work Backward
13. Use Cases
14. Solve an Equation
15. Look for a Formula
16. Do a Simulation
17. Use a Model

17-1. The surface of a cube is painted red. The cube is then cut into equal sized smaller cubes, 24 of which have only one red face. How many of the smaller cubes have two red faces? No red faces?

17-2. Sandy has a collection of nickels and dimes. The nickels can be put into piles so that the number of nickels in each pile is the same as the number of piles. Also, the dimes can be put into piles so that the number of dimes in each pile is the same as the number of piles. Which of the following could not be the total value of Sandy's coin collection?

a. $3.40    b. $5.35    c. $3.00    d. $6.05

17-3. Assume that there are more turkeys in Minnesota than there are feathers on any one turkey. Show that at least two of these turkeys must have the same number of feathers, given that each turkey has at least one feather.

17-4. How can the faces of two cubes be labeled with whole numbers so that, when they are tossed, the sum can be any number from 1 through 12 and the probability of getting each sum is the same?

**18**

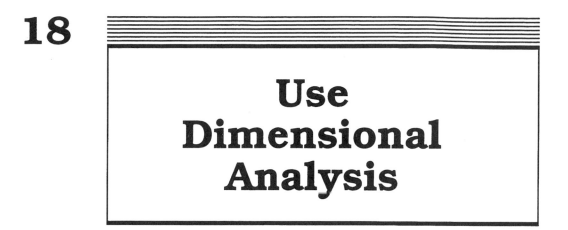

# Use Dimensional Analysis

In a horse race, Kentucky Prancer ran 6 furlongs in 1 minute and 6 seconds. Express Kentucky Prancer's rate in miles per hour and in feet per second. (Note: 1 mile = 8 furlongs.)

## SOLUTION

Problem:   In a horse race, Kentucky Prancer ran 6 furlongs in 1 minute and 6 seconds. Express Kentucky Prancer's rate in miles per hour and in feet per second. (Note: 1 mi = 8 fur.)

Solution:   First, 6 seconds = $6 \, \cancel{sec} \times \dfrac{1 \, min}{60 \, \cancel{sec}} = 0.1$ minutes, so

1 minute and 6 seconds = 1.1 minutes

$$\frac{6 \, fur}{1.1 \, min} = \frac{6 \, \cancel{fur}}{1.1 \, \cancel{min}} \times \frac{1 \, mi}{8 \, \cancel{fur}} \times \frac{60 \, \cancel{min}}{1 \, hr}$$

$$= \frac{6 \times 60}{1.1 \times 8} \, \frac{mi}{hr} \approx 40.91 \frac{mi}{hr}$$

Therefore, 6 furlongs/1.1 minutes is about 40.91 miles/hour.

$$\frac{40.91 \, mi}{1 \, hr} = \frac{40.91 \, \cancel{mi}}{1 \, \cancel{hr}} \times \frac{1 \, \cancel{hr}}{60 \, \cancel{min}} \times \frac{1 \, \cancel{min}}{60 \, sec} \times \frac{5280 \, ft}{1 \, \cancel{mi}}$$

$$= \frac{40.91 \times 5280}{60 \times 60} \, \frac{ft}{sec} \approx 60 \, \frac{ft}{sec}$$

Therefore, 6 furlongs/1.1 minutes is about 60.00 feet/second

a.   How many miles are there in 1000 furlongs?
b.   Some horse races are 5.5 furlongs. How many yards is that?
c.   How many feet are there in 6 furlongs?

## DISCUSSION

The Use Dimensional Analysis strategy is helpful when it is necessary to convert a measurement from one unit to another. In applying the strategy, we use unit ratios equivalent to 1, e.g. 5280 feet/1 mile = 1. The following example shows how dimensional analysis can be used to convert a growth rate of 0.37 inches per week to feet per year.

$$\frac{0.37 \, in}{1 \, wk} = \frac{0.37 \, \cancel{in}}{1 \, \cancel{wk}} \times \frac{52 \, \cancel{wk}}{1 \, yr} \times \frac{1 \, ft}{12 \, \cancel{in}} = \frac{0.37 \times 52}{12} \, \frac{ft}{yr} \approx 1.603 \, \frac{ft}{yr}$$

## CLUES

The Use Dimensional Analysis strategy may be appropriate when:

*   Units of measure are involved.
*   The problem involves physical quantities.
*   Conversions are required.

## PRACTICE PROBLEMS

---

Problem: Under normal conditions, the atmospheric pressure at sea level is about 14.7 pounds per square inch. What is the pressure in grams per square centimeter?

---

Solution: Use Dimensional Analysis

$1 \text{ kg} \approx 2.2 \text{ pounds}$

$1 \text{ in} = 2.54 \text{ cm, so } 1 \text{ in}^2 = (2.54)^2 \text{ cm}^2 = 6.4516 \text{ cm}^2$

$$\frac{14.7 \text{ lb}}{1 \text{ in}^2} \approx \frac{14.7 \text{ lb}}{1 \text{ in}^2} \times \frac{1 \text{ in}^2}{6.45 \text{ cm}^2} \times \frac{1 \text{ kg}}{2.2 \text{ lb}} \times \frac{1000 \text{ g}}{1 \text{ kg}}$$

$$\approx \frac{14.7 \times 1000}{6.45 \times 2.2} \frac{\text{g}}{\text{cm}^2}$$

$$\approx 1035.94 \frac{\text{g}}{\text{cm}^2}$$

Therefore, 14.7 pounds per sq. in. is about 1036 grams per $\text{cm}^2$.

---

18–A. Find the exact number of meters in one mile using the fact that 1 inch equals 2.54 centimeters.

18–B. The fuel consumption of a certain car is 24 miles per gallon. How many kilometers per liter is this? (1 mile $\approx$ 1.61 kilometers and 1 liter $\approx$ 1.06 quarts.)

# MIXED STRATEGY PRACTICE

PROBLEM-SOLVING
STRATEGIES

1. Guess and Test
2. Use a Variable
3. Draw a Picture
4. Look for a Pattern
5. Make a List
6. Solve a Simpler Problem
7. Draw a Diagram
8. Use Direct Reasoning
9. Use Indirect Reasoning
10. Use Properties of Numbers
11. Solve an Equivalent Problem
12. Work Backward
13. Use Cases
14. Solve an Equation
15. Look for a Formula
16. Do a Simulation
17. Use a Model
18. Use Dimensional Analysis

18–1.   A certain brand of laundry soap is sold as either a liquid or a powder. A survey by the company that makes the soap revealed the following information.

* $\frac{2}{7}$ of those interviewed do not use the liquid.

* $\frac{1}{3}$ do not use the powder.

* 183 use both the liquid and the powder.

* $\frac{1}{5}$ do not use this brand of soap.

How many people were interviewed?

18–2.   Find an efficient way to decide which of the numbers below is a term in the sequence 7, 16, 25, 34, 43, ...

1,200,000,301          1,100,201,301

18–3.   On a balance scale, 3 red cubes and 1 white cube balance 3 blue cubes. Also, 1 red cube and 3 blue cubes balance 3 white cubes. How many blue cubes will balance 5 white cubes?

18–4.   Mary has two 20 ounce cups full of water. She also has an empty 8 ounce cup and an empty 14 ounce cup. Using only these four cups, she wants to end up with exactly 6 ounces of water in each of the smaller cups. Without spilling a drop, how can this be done in six steps?

# 19

# Identify Subgoals

Six men and two boys want to cross a river using a small raft that will carry either two boys or one man. How many times must the raft cross the river in order to get everybody to the other side?

## SOLUTION

Problem:   Six men and two boys want to cross a river using a small raft that will carry either two boys or one man.  How many times must the raft cross the river in order to get everybody to the other side?

Solution:  A subgoal is to find the number of crossings needed to get one man across the river and return the raft to the starting point.

The two boys cross.  One boy brings the raft back.  One man crosses.  The other boy brings the raft back to the starting point.  Now the raft is where it started and one man is across the river (4 crossings).

Therefore, it will take 24 (4 × 6) trips to move the six men across the river and have the raft back at the starting point. One additional crossing will be needed to get the two boys to the other side. Hence, it will take 25 crossings to get everyone to the other side of the river.

a.   How many crossings of the river would be needed if there were six men and four boys to start with?
b.   Would it be possible for six men and one boy to cross the river under the conditions stated in the problem?  Why or why not?

## DISCUSSION

Some problems can best be solved by first identifying one or more intermediate conditions or "subgoals" whose results may lead to a solution to the original problem.  For example, in trying to find the sum of the numbers in the sequence 11, 16, 21, 36, 41, ... , 206, a subgoal is to find the number of terms in the sequence, namely 40.  With this information, we can then proceed to show that the sum is 20 × 217, or 4,340.  Explain why 20 × 217 yields the correct answer.

## CLUES

The Identify Subgoals  strategy may be appropriate when:

*    A problem can be broken down into a series of simpler problems.
*    The statement of the problem is very long and complex.
*    You can say  "If I only knew ..., then I could solve the problem."
*    There is a simple, intermediate step that would be useful.
*    There is other information that you wished the problem contained.

## PRACTICE PROBLEMS

Problem:   Find the area of a regular hexagon that has a perimeter of 12 centimeters.

Solution:   Identify Subgoals

A regular hexagon can be partitioned into six equilateral triangles.  Therefore, a subgoal is to find the area of an equilateral triangle whose sides are 2 centimeters long.

Area of the triangle = $\frac{1}{2} \times 2 \times \sqrt{3} = \sqrt{3}$ cm$^2$.

Hence, the area of the hexagon is $6\sqrt{3}$ cm$^2$.

$h^2 + 1 = 4$

$h = \sqrt{3}$

19–A.   The figure shown has a regular octagon adjacent to a regular pentagon.  Find the measure of angle ABC.

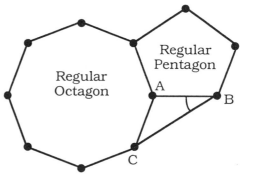

19–B.   How many ways are there to travel from X to Y if you must go either up or to the right along the lines?

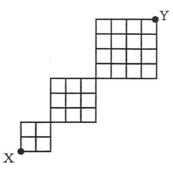

## MIXED STRATEGY PRACTICE

1. Guess and Test
2. Use a Variable
3. Draw a Picture
4. Look for a Pattern
5. Make a List
6. Solve a Simpler Problem
7. Draw a Diagram
8. Use Direct Reasoning
9. Use Indirect Reasoning
10. Use Properties of Numbers
11. Solve an Equivalent Problem
12. Work Backward
13. Use Cases
14. Solve an Equation
15. Look for a Formula
16. Do a Simulation
17. Use a Model
18. Use Dimensional Analysis
19. Identify Subgoals

19–1.  Tom and Scott ran a 400 meter race. When Scott was at the finish line, Tom was 20 meters behind. The next day they decided to run the same race, but Scott started 21 meters behind the starting line. If each one again runs at the previous rate, where will Scott be when Tom is 1 meter from the finish line? Who will win the race?

19–2.  A baseball coach paid $81 for some jerseys and caps. If the jerseys cost $7 each and the caps cost $3 each, which of the following could be the ratio of jerseys to caps purchased?

5:4     4:3     3:2     5:3     7:3

19–3.  ABCD is a parallelogram. Show that if $\overline{AC}$ is a diagonal, then the area of region X must be equal to the area of region Y.

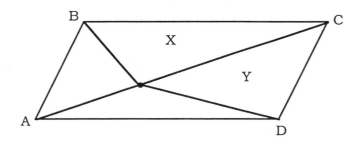

19–4.  Find the number of feet in the perimeter of a rectangular playing field given that the area is 312 square yards, the longest side, in feet, is 3 less than a perfect square, and the length and width are whole numbers.

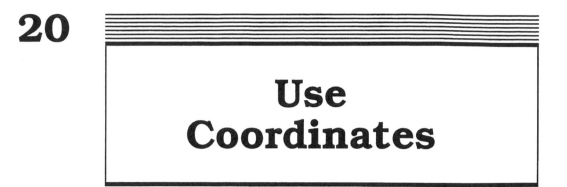

# 20

# Use
# Coordinates

A scout troop is trying to find a secret message that is hidden at corner B of a field which is a parallelogram ABCD. Point A is 6 meters north and 30 meters east of the flagpole, point C is 54 meters north and 12 meters west of the pole, and point D is 18 meters north and 42 meters east of the pole. What is the location of the secret message?

## SOLUTION

Problem:   A scout troop is trying to find a secret message that is hidden at corner B of a field which is a parallelogram ABCD.  Point A is 6 meters north and 30 meters east of the flagpole, point C is 54 meters north and 12 meters west of the pole, and point D is 18 meters north and 42 meters east of the pole.  What is the location of the secret message?

Solution:   Suppose the flagpole is at (0, 0).

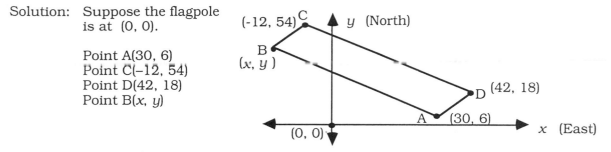

Point A(30, 6)
Point C(-12, 54)
Point D(42, 18)
Point B(x, y)

Since ABCD is a parallelogram, its opposite sides must be parallel.  This means that the slope of $\overline{AB}$ equals the slope of $\overline{CD}$, and the slope of $\overline{AD}$ equals the slope of $\overline{BC}$.  Using this information, it can be shown that the hidden message is 42 meters north and 24 meters west of the flagpole.

a.   What is the slope of $\overline{AD}$?  $\overline{BC}$?  $\overline{CD}$?
b.   One way to solve this problem is to find the values of $x$ and $y$ when $(y - 54)/(x + 12) = 1$ and $(y - 6)/(x - 30) = -2/3$.  Show why this is the case and then find the values for $x$ and $y$.
c.   Show how this problem can be solved without using equations.

## DISCUSSION

A two–dimensional coordinate system with the origin, (0,0), conveniently located is often helpful in solving geometric problems.  For example, in trying to show that the diagonals of a rhombus are perpendicular bisectors of each other, we can start by representing its four vertices as shown.  Then, using slope and midpoint formulas, we can solve the problem.

Note: $c^2 = a^2 - b^2$

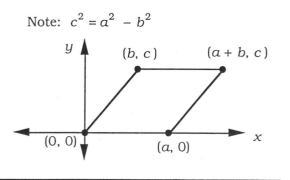

## CLUES

The Use Coordinates  strategy may be appropriate when:

*   A problem can be represented using two variables.
*   A geometry problem cannot easily be solved by using traditional Euclidean methods.
*   Finding representations of lines or conic sections.
*   A problem involves slope, parallel lines, perpendicular lines, etc.
*   The location of a geometric shape with respect to other shapes is important.
*   A problem involves maps.

## PRACTICE PROBLEMS

Problem:   Given a pentagon ABCDE.
Also, ABCD is a rectangle.

Show that $AE^2 + CE^2 = BE^2 + DE^2$

Solution:   Use Coordinates

Using coordinates, we can position the
pentagon as shown.

$$AE^2 = x^2 + y^2$$
$$CE^2 = (a - x)^2 + (b - y)^2$$

$$BE^2 = x^2 + (b - y)^2$$
$$DE^2 = (a - x)^2 + y^2$$

Therefore, $AE^2 + CE^2 = BE^2 + DE^2$.

20–A.   Find the area of the quadrilateral ABCD which has its vertices at points A (–2, 1), B (2, 3), C (1, 1), and D (3, –1).

20–B.   Suppose triangle ABC has vertices $(r, s)$, $(r + 1, s + 7)$, and $(r - 3, s + 4)$. Show that it is an isosceles right triangle and find its area.

# MIXED STRATEGY PRACTICE

**PROBLEM-SOLVING STRATEGIES**

1. Guess and Test
2. Use a Variable
3. Draw a Picture
4. Look for a Pattern
5. Make a List
6. Solve a Simpler Problem
7. Draw a Diagram
8. Use Direct Reasoning
9. Use Indirect Reasoning
10. Use Properties of Numbers
11. Solve an Equivalent Problem
12. Work Backward
13. Use Cases
14. Solve an Equation
15. Look for a Formula
16. Do a Simulation
17. Use a Model
18. Use Dimensional Analysis
19. Identify Subgoals
20. Use Coordinates

20–1. While riding a bicycle from her home to Janesville, Jane traveled 1/2 the distance at 18 mph, 1/3 the distance at 8 mph, and 1/6 the distance at 3 mph. What was Jane's average speed for the trip?

20–2. A taxi, a limousine, and a bus travel from the airport to the Regency Hotel 24 hours a day. A taxi leaves every 15 minutes, a limousine leaves every 28 minutes, and a bus leaves every 40 minutes. If each type of vehicle leaves the airport at 9 A.M. on Monday, at what time will they leave the airport together on the following Friday?

20–3. There are two sets of railroad tracks between Kenyon and Riverdale. Every hour, on the hour, a train leaves each city for the other city. The trains always travel at the same rate and the trip from one city to the other takes 5 hours. How many trains will be met by a train traveling from Kenyon to Riverdale?

20–4. Suppose you have two pieces of rope that have different lengths. Show how to cut one of the pieces so that one of the resulting 3 pieces has a length which is the same as the average length of the other two pieces.

# 21

# Use Symmetry

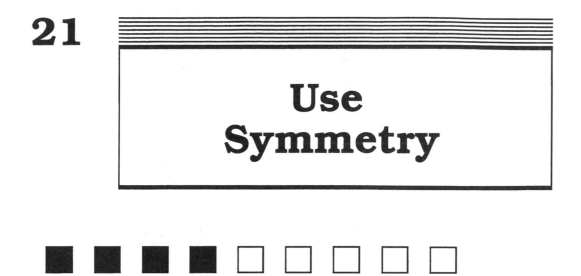

How many different ways can the above squares be arranged as a 3 by 3 square which has exactly one line of symmetry?

## SOLUTION

Problem:    How many different ways can the above squares be arranged as a 3 by 3 square which has exactly one line of symmetry?

Solution:   The ten 3 by 3 arrays shown below represent all the different ways where there is exactly one line of symmetry.

a.   Draw the line of symmetry in each 3 by 3 array above.
b.   Is it possible to arrange the nine squares so that there are exactly 2 lines of symmetry? Exactly 4 lines of symmetry?

## DISCUSSION

Some problems can more easily be analyzed by using symmetry. Geometrical symmetry may involve slides, turns, or flips. For example, the results of the first two plays on the tic-tac–toe boards shown below are equivalent by rotational symmetry.

Numerical symmetries can also be helpful in solving certain types of problems. For example, if a whole number has an even number of digits and is symmetric, such as 123,321, then it is divisible by 11. Explain why.

## CLUES

The Use Symmetry  strategy may be appropriate when:

*    Geometry problems involve transformations.
*    Interchanging values does not change the representation of the problem.
*    Symmetry limits the number of cases that need to be considered.
*    Pictures or algebraic procedures appear to be symmetric.

## PRACTICE PROBLEMS

Problem:   Suppose triangle ABC has its vertices at A (1, –1), B (4, –2), and C (–1, –4).  Find the vertices of its mirror image when it is reflected about the line which has a slope of 1 and passes through the point (3, 4).

Solution:   Use Symmetry

The figure at right shows the mirror image,  triangle A'B'C', of triangle ABC reflected  about the line.  Explain how the coordinates  of A', B', and  C'  can be determined from the  given information.

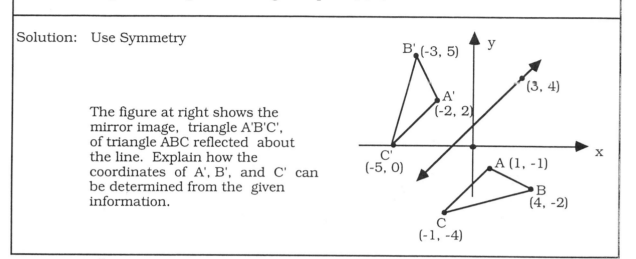

21–A.   Two players take turns placing the same color marker on one of the dots shown on the playing board below.  The winner is the first player that completes a string of 3 consecutive dots covered by a marker.  Find a strategy so that the first player will always win.

21–B.   Suppose a ball is placed at point X on the pool table represented below.  A player wants to shoot the ball so that it goes into the corner pocket P after rebounding off cushion *r* and then off cushion *s*.  Locate the points where the ball must hit each cushion.

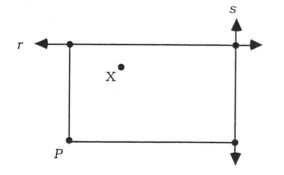

# MIXED STRATEGY PRACTICE

PROBLEM-SOLVING
STRATEGIES

1. Guess and Test
2. Use a Variable
3. Draw a Picture
4. Look for a Pattern
5. Make a List
6. Solve a Simpler Problem
7. Draw a Diagram
8. Use Direct Reasoning
9. Use Indirect Reasoning
10. Use Properties of Numbers
11. Solve an Equivalent Problem
12. Work Backward
13. Use Cases
14. Solve an Equation
15. Look for a Formula
16. Do a Simulation
17. Use a Model
18. Use Dimensional Analysis
19. Identify Subgoals
20. Use Coordinates
21. Use Symmetry

21-1. Find the measure of each angle of a regular polygon that has 20 diagonals.

21-2. To estimate the number of fish in Lake George, 800 fish were caught, tagged, and then returned to the lake. Later that week, 150 fish were caught, 6 of which were tagged. Use this information to estimate the fish population of the lake.

21-3. Ralph paid $1.87 for some candy bars at a "20% to 40% off" sale. How many candy bars did he buy if they regularly sell for 25 cents each?

21-4. A horse is tied to the corner of a 30 foot by 50 foot barn with a 60 foot rope. If the horse can graze everywhere outside of the barn that the rope allows it to reach, what is the grazing area?

# ADDITIONAL PRACTICE PROBLEMS

## Guess and Test

1. I am a whole number between 40,000 and 50,000. When I am divided by 2, the answer is a perfect square. When I am divided by 3, the answer is a perfect cube. Who am I?

   *46,656*

2. A rectangular room has an area of 665 square feet. Its length is three less than twice its width. What are the dimensions of the room?

## Use a Variable

1. Is it possible for two or more consecutive odd counting numbers to have a sum of 343? If so, find the numbers. If not, show why not.

2. Write six consecutive odd counting numbers. __ __ __ __ __ __
   Verify that the sum of the smallest and largest is half the sum of the other four numbers. Show why this must always be true.

## Draw a Picture

1. Glen runs 10 meters in the same time that Leo runs 8 meters. One day they ran around a 400-meter circular track. They started at the same place at the same time and they ran in opposite directions. What was Glen's location on the track when Leo passed the starting line the third time?

2. Tortino's Pizza, located on the 2nd floor of an office building, guarantees 20-minute delivery. On a certain Monday, four orders were received between 11:45 AM and 11:55 AM. Shortly after, with four pizzas in hand, Fast Eddy delivered a pizza at an office located on the middle floor after which he went up 5 floors to deliver a second pizza. He then went down 9 floors to deliver a pizza. From there he took an elevator up 17 floors to the top floor where he delivered the last pizza. How may floors are in the office building given that Fast Eddy delivered the last pizza at 12:10 PM?

## Look for a Pattern

1.    1=1     4=1+3     9=1+3+5     16=1+3+5+7     25=1+3+5+7+9

   Use the pattern suggested above to help you find the missing numbers.

   a. _____ = 1 + 3 + 5 + 7 + ... + 79.

   b. 8,100 = 1 + 3 + 5 + 7 + 9 + ... + _____ .

   c. 3,136 is the sum of the first _____ odd whole numbers.

   d. 7 + 9 + 11 + 13 + ... + 97 + 99 = _____ .

2. 
   | A | 1 | | | |
   |---|----|----|----|----|
   | B | 3 | 5 | | |
   | C | 7 | 9 | 11 | |
   | D | 13 | 15 | 17 | 19 |
   | . | | | | |
   | . | | | | |
   | . | | | | |
   | Z | | | | |

   a. Find the sum of the numbers in set J.

   b. What is the first number in set Z?

   c. What is the average of the numbers in set T?

   d. Which set has numbers whose sum is 8,000?

## Make a List

1.  How many different ways can nine dimes be placed into three piles given that each pile must end up with at least 20 cents?

2.  A company wants to construct a box that will hold exactly 200 one-inch cubes. Find the dimensions of all possible boxes. Which size box do you think the company should make? Why?

## Solve a Simpler Problem

1.  Find the sum of the digits in the answer for each problem below.

    a.  55,555,555 x 999,999,999

    b.  $666,666,666,666,667^2$

2.  Find the average of the first:

    a.  999 counting numbers.

    b.  999 even natural numbers.

    c.  999 odd whole numbers.

    d.  999 numbers in the set {4,8,12,16,...}.

## Draw a Diagram

1.  In a class of 48 college students, 16 are neither men nor left-handed. Thirty are men, and 41 of the students are not left-handed. How many women in the class are left-handed?

2.  How many 3-digit even numbers less than 400 contain only the digits 3, 4, 6, 8, and 9 given that all of the digits must be different?

## Use Direct Reasoning

1.  Three men named Bob, Ken, and John are in a boat. Bob always tells the truth, Ken tells the truth sometimes, and John never tells the truth. The man in the middle said, "I'm Ken," the man at the front of the boat said, "Bob is in the middle," and the man at the back said, "John is at the front end." Which one is in the middle of the boat?

2.  Use the given clues to find the number represented by each letter.

    * Each is a different 1-digit whole number.
    * All corner numbers are even.             A      B      C
    * The product of B and E is 15.
    * Half the sum of C and F is 3.            D      E      F
    * C is 2 less than D.
    * E is greater than C.

## Use Indirect Reasoning

1. If AB and BA represent 2- digit counting numbers where A is greater than B, show that AB divided by BA cannot equal 2.

2. The counting numbers 1 through 16 can be placed in a 4 by 4 square array so that the sum of the numbers in each row, column, and diagonal is the same. Show why the four corner numbers cannot all be odd.

## Use Properties of Numbers

1. Each of the following represents a 6-digit number that is a multiple of 12, but not a multiple of 9. Find all possible values for K for each problem.

   Note: In each problem, K must be the same digit.
   a. 1K31K4            b. 5KKK28            c. 10KK5K

2. What is the smallest counting number, which when divided by any of the numbers in the set {2, 3, 4, . . ., 9, 10}, leaves a remainder of 1?

## Solve an Equivalent Problem

1. Mario's pizza shop offers small, medium, and large pizzas. You can order a plain cheese pizza or a pizza with one or more of eight toppings. How many different ways can a pizza be ordered at Mario's?

2. How many different line segments can be drawn between 9 equally spaced points on a circle? Between N equally spaced points?

## Work Backward

1. Ted has a collection of stamps. He gave his sister one more than half. Then he gave his brother 3 less than half of the remaining stamps. How many stamps did Ted have in his original collection if he ended up with 19 stamps?

2. Della and Tess played a game in which they take turns selecting one of the following numbers: 1 2 3 4. After a number is selected, it is added to the sum of all numbers previously selected. To win the game, a player must get exactly 41. If Della goes first, show how she can be a sure winner.

## Use Cases

1. When will $(X^2 - XY)$ be negative given that X and Y are integers?

2. Bob, Ted, and Paul have the same birthday. Ted is now half Bob's age. Five years ago Paul was one-third of Bob's age then. Which one will be 14 years old on his next birthday?

## Solve an Equation

1. While telling his friends about the big fish he caught during his Canadian fishing trip, Stan said, "Ten pounds more than half its weight is 2 pounds more than its weight." What was the weight of his prize catch?

2. Select two different numbers. Write one of the numbers above A and the other above B. Then find the numbers C through J by adding the preceding two numbers. The sum of all numbers (A through J) should be 11 times the number above G. Verify.

$$\overline{A} \quad \overline{B} \quad \overline{C} \quad \overline{D} \quad \overline{E} \quad \overline{F} \quad \overline{G} \quad \overline{H} \quad \overline{I} \quad \overline{J}$$

Show why $11 \times G$ must always equal the sum $A + B + C + D + E + F + G + H + I + J$.

## Look for a Formula

1.  How many rectangles, of all sizes, are there on a $20 \times 20$ square grid?

2.  Find the Nth term in each sequence shown below when:
    N is an odd number.                N is an even number.

    a.  4, 8, 16, 16, 64, 24, 256, 32, 1024, 40, . . .

    b.  8, 4, 16, 16, 24, 36, 32, 64, 40, 100, . . .

## Do a Simulation

1.  Start by placing a marker on X. Then toss a coin 5 times. Each time it lands heads up, move 1 space to the right and each time it lands tails up, move 1 space to the left. If at any time during the 5 tosses your marker lands on C, you lose the game. Otherwise, you win.

    Which of the following best represents your chance of winning the game?
    0.1      0.3      0.5      0.7      0.9

    ```
    -- --- --      ----- --     -- --- --     ---- --     ----- --      -- --- --
         C                                  X                                  C
    ```

2.  Two dice are tossed. The numbers that appear on top are then used to form the largest possible 2-digit number. Explain how a random-digit table can be used to estimate the probability of ending up with a number greater than 41. Then use your method (50 trials) to help you decide which of the following is closest to the exact answer.

    0.3      0.5      0.7      0.9

## Use a Model

1. Show how 4 red, 4 white, 4 blue, and 4 yellow chips can be placed on a 4 by 4 array of 16 squares so that no row, column, or diagonal ends up with two chips of the same color.

2. An open top box of height 8 cm has a 6 cm by 12 cm rectangular base. If the box is filled with 1 x 1 x 1 centimeter cubes, how many faces of the cubes touch either a side or the bottom of the box?

## Use Dimensional Analysis

1. Which of the following numbers best represents the largest number of cubes, each of which has a surface area of 24 square centimeters, that can be put into a cubical box of volume 64 cubic inches? 100 125 150 175 200 (1 inch = 2.54 centimeters)

2. Starting at the same time, Carl and Brian ran around a 400-meter track in opposite directions. Carl's average rate was 17 meters for every two seconds and Brian's average rate was 6 yards per second. How long, to the nearest second, did it take before they met on the other side of the track?

## Identify Subgoals

1. The sixteen consecutive whole numbers from 8 through 23 can be written in a 4 x 4 square array so that the sum of the numbers in each row, column, and diagonal is the same. Find the missing numbers in the 4 x 4 array.

| 22 |    | 16 | 11 |
|----|----|----|----|
|    | 10 |    |    |
| 15 |    | 9  | 18 |
| 8  |    |    |    |

2. How many different trapezoids are there in the below figure given that all the horizontal line segments are parallel and no other segments are parallel?

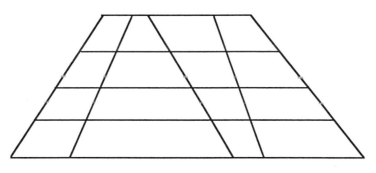

## Use Coordinates

1. Suppose triangle ABC is a right triangle where angle B is a right angle and (20,15) is the midpoint of its hypotenuse. Find its area given that point B is located at (8,10).

2. Find the area and perimeter of triangle ABC with vertices A(-1, 3), B(2, 7), and C(5, 3).

## Use Symmetry

1.  Parallelogram ABCD has vertices A(4, 6), B(7, 10), C(23, 10), and D(20, 6).  Find the vertices of the parallelogram's final location if it is reflected about the line y = -1 and then rotated 180 degrees about the origin (0, 0).

2.  How many different ways can 5 pennies be placed into the following 3 by 3 square so that the 5-penny arrangement has:

    a.  at least one line of symmetry?          b.  180 degree rotational symmetry?

    Note:   Two figures are not different if one of the figures can be rotated 180 degrees to form the other figure.

## ADDITIONAL MIXED STRATEGY PRACTICE

1. Eight 4-inch by 6-inch pictures are to be mounted on a 21-inch by 31-inch rectangular sheet. Show how this can be done if the distance between the pictures must be the same as the distance from their edges.

2. Find the difference between the largest 5-digit perfect cube and the smallest 4-digit perfect square.

3. The total weight of a box and its contents of two dozen identical red chips is 77 grams. After 9 of the chips are removed, the total weight of the box and the remaining red chips is 59 grams. What is the total weight when the box contains only one red chip?

4. Troy, Dan, Carlos, and Willie are married to Melissa, Laura, Shelly, and Juanita. Use the below clues to determine who is married to whom.

   * Shelly is Dan's sister.       * Juanita's husband is an only child.
   * Melissa is married to Carlos.    * Willie is not married to Shelly.

5.  A can of cola and a can of root beer are each exactly half full. Two ounces of cola are poured into the can of root beer. Then two ounces of the mixture in the root beer can are poured into the cola can. Is there now more cola in the root beer can or more root beer in the cola can? Explain.

6.  Ten red, 9 white, 8 blue, and 7 yellow chips are in a box. Without looking, what is the smallest number of chips that you must take out of the box to be sure of ending up with at least:
    a. 2 of the same color?      b. 4 of the same color?      c. 6 of the same color?

7.  Nadine has a collection of dimes and quarters worth $4.00. Which of the following numbers cannot be the total number of coins in her collection?
    
    18          25          28          36          37

8.  Find the 999th term in each of the following sequences:
    a. 2 4 5 6 2 4 5 6 2 4 5 6 ...
    b. 1 4 2 8 5 7 1 4 2 8 5 7 1 4 2 8 5 7 ...

9.  Pencils and pens are on sale for 96 cents a dozen and 3 for 51 cents, respectively. Karen bought some of each. How many pencils did she buy if her change for a $5 bill was $2.53?

10. Tyrone sold 100 vehicles (cars, vans and trucks) last year. He sold 58 used vehicles, 60 cars, 13 used vans, and two-thirds of the 21 trucks he sold were used. How many of the new vehicles sold by Tyrone were either cars or vans?

11. Of the four children in the Jackson family, Barb is 2 years younger than Ken, Sam is half of Barb's age, Barb is 7 years older than Linda and the sum of their ages is 30. Find the age of each child given that the difference between the ages of their parents is 3 years.

12. Juanita has 16 coins consisting of nickels, dimes, and quarters. Fourteen of her coins are not nickels and all but seven of her coins are quarters. How much money does she have?

13. Jodi has a collection of nickels, dimes, and quarters worth $2.00. If the nickels were dimes and the dimes were nickels, the value of the coins would be $1.70. How many nickels could Jodi have?

14. Ken can beat Jim by 100 meters in a 1,000-meter race, and Jim can beat Bob by 10 meters in a 100-meter race. If both run at the given rate, by how many meters will Ken beat Bob in a 1,000-meter race?

15. How many different rectangles are in the figure shown below?

16. Find the 3-digit number that satisfies all conditions stated below.
    * The sum of the digits is 13.
    * The product of the digits is greater than 60.
    * The sum of the tens and hundreds digits is less than the ones digit.
    * The number is between 300 and 400.

17.  In how many different ways can 99 dimes be placed into two piles given that the total value of the coins in each pile must be at least 30 cents?

18.  Find the sum of the digits in the smallest 9-digit number that is both a perfect square and a perfect cube.

19.  The EE-ZZ Cleaning Company offers the following salary options to its salespeople.
     Option A:  $500 a month plus $30 for each vacuum cleaner sold
     Option B:  $300 a month plus $50 for each vacuum cleaner sold
     Under what conditions is it better to select option B?

20.  In a group of cows, ducks, and turkeys, the number of legs is 44 more than the number of heads.  What is the largest number of cows that could be in this group of animals?

21. Find an efficient way to decide which of the following numbers is equal to 14 factorial.
    Note:  14! = 14 factorial = $14 \times 13 \times 12 \times 11 \times ... \times 3 \times 2 \times 1$

    a. 87178291400        b. 87178291200        c. 8717829120        d. 871782912000

22. a  How many games must be played to determine a champion in the 64-team NCAA
       single elimination basketball tournament?
    b. How many games are played in the Pac Ten Conference, if each team plays all the
       other teams at home and away?
    c. What is the least number of games that must be played to determine a champion
       in an 8-team double elimination tournament?

23. I am a 2-digit number between 21 and 61.  My ones digit is a multiple of my tens digit and
    I am five less than a perfect square.  Who am I?

24. Three candles of equal length were all lit at 11 p.m.  Candle X takes 12 hours to burn out,
    candle Y takes 8 hours to burn out, and candle Z takes 6 hours to burn out.

    a. At what time will candle Y burn out?
    b. At what time will candle X be twice as long as candle Z?
    c. At what time will candle Y be half as long as candle X?
    d. At what time will candle Z be 80% as long as candle X?

25.  Brenda leaves for work at 6:30 a.m. every weekday.  If she averages 8 miles per hour to work, she will be 1/2 hour late.  At a rate of 24 miles per hour, she will be one hour early.  How far is it from Brenda's home to where she works?

26.  Use the clues below to help you find my telephone number.

$$\underset{1}{\_\,\_\,\_\,\_}\ \ \underset{2}{\_\,\_\,\_\,\_}\ \ \underset{3}{\_\,\_\,\_\,\_}\ \ \underset{4}{\_\,\_\,\_\,\_}\ \ \underset{5}{\_\,\_\,\_\,\_}\ \ \underset{6}{\_\,\_\,\_\,\_}\ \ \underset{7}{\_\,\_\,\_\,\_}$$

* The seven digits are all prime numbers.
* The 1st, 4th, and 5th digits are all even.
* The 2nd and 3rd digits are factors of 35.
* The 6th digit is 4 less than the 7th digit.
* The sum of the digits is neither 28 nor 30.

27.  The difference between the squares of two consecutive odd counting numbers is equal  to the largest 3-digit multiple of 8.  What are the numbers?

28.  A farmer fenced in a rectangular field of perimeter 340 meters.  He then divided the field into two equal areas by constructing a fence diagonally across the field.  All of the fence posts are 10 meters apart and the width of the field is 50 meters.  How many fence posts did the farmer use?

29.   Of the 90 cars in a parking lot, 34 are neither 4-door nor compact cars. There are 35 compact cars and 43 of the cars have 4 doors. How many of the 4-door cars in the parking lot are not compact cars?

30.   Use the given clues to find the number represented by each letter.

      * All are different counting numbers less than 100.      **A**     **B**     **C**
      * Each corner number is a square less than 35.
      * B + E equals the first prime number after 19.      **D**     **E**     **F**
      * A + D = F = A + B + C.
      * D is half of E.

31.   A half mile long train is traveling at 45 mph while entering a one mile long tunnel at 1:15 p.m. How long, in seconds, will it take until the end of the last car in the train first reaches daylight?

32.   Gina's father said that she would get $130 and a new bicycle if she mows the lawn 30 times. After mowing the lawn 20 times, she got a new bike and $50. If this represents the total amount Gina has earned up to that time, how much did the bike cost?

33.    Three views of a single cube are shown.

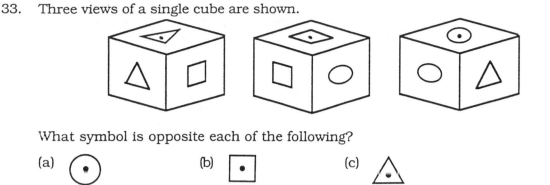

What symbol is opposite each of the following?

(a) ●        (b) ▪        (c) △

34.    How many numbers between 99 and 999 are divisible by 4, 6, and 9?

35.    A 16 inch by 30 inch rectangular sheet is made into an open top box by first cutting identical squares from each corner and then folding up the sides. What is the largest possible volume of the box if the edge of each cut-out square, in inches, is a whole number?

36.    Bill ate half the cookies in a cookie jar. Amy then ate 1/4 of the remaining cookies. Then Karia ate 1/3 of the cookies left. Ken and Juanita then shared the remaining cookies equally. If Juanita got 2 cookies, how many cookies were there before Bill found the cookie jar?

37.  A 3-member committee is to be randomly selected from a group of 4 girls and 6 boys. Explain how a random number table can be used to estimate the probability that the committee will be either all boys or all girls.

38.  Cal gave Brad and Jenny as many sports cards as each of them already has. Then Brad gave Cal and Jenny as many sports cards as each of them presently has. Finally, Jenny gave Cal and Brad as many sports cards as each had at that time. If they all ended up with 64 cards, how many did each one have at the start?

39.  The gauge on a water tank shows 5/8 full. After 21 more gallons were drained, the gauge showed 1/3 full. How many gallons of water were in the tank when it showed 1/2 full?

40.  Two boxes A and B each contain some nickels and some dimes. The ratios of dimes to nickels in A and B are in 1 to 3 and 5 to 4, respectively. The total value of the dimes in both boxes is $2.90. Suppose all coins that are in box A are put into box B. What ratio of dimes to nickels could now be in box B?

41. The figure shown at right has an area of 40 square units. Explain why it is not possible to completely cover the figure with twenty 1 by 2 unit rectangles.

42. There are between 50 and 100 books on a bookshelf. One-ninth ot the books are workbooks and 25% are textbooks. How many books are on the shelf?

43. A game at the state fair consists of two boxes labeled X and Y; 9 white balls, and 5 black balls. A player is allowed to place the balls into the boxes in any way. A coin is then tossed. If it lands heads up, a ball is selected from box X. Otherwise, it must be selected from box Y. To win a prize, the ball selected must be white. How should the balls be placed into the boxes so that the player has the best possible chance of winning a prize? Explain.

44. Suppose N is a 1-digit counting number. Given that the ones digit of $N^{97}$ is N, what are the possible values for N?

45.  The whole numbers 1 through 25 can be written in a
     5 by 5 square array so that the sum of each row, column,
     and diagonal is the same.  Show why 1, 2, 3, and 4 cannot
     all be corner numbers.

46.  Find the measure of the smallest angle between the hands of a clock when it shows:
        a. 3:40 a.m.              b. 2:20 p.m.

47.  Box X contains 8 chips marked as              Box Y contains 4 chips marked as
     follows: 1 1 2 2 3 3 4 4                       follows: 1 2 3 4

     Player X randomly selects two                  Player Y randomly selects one
     chips from box X and finds the                 chip from box Y and finds the
     product of the numbers selected.               square of the number selected.

     The player with the largest answer wins the game.  Which player, X or Y, would you like
     to be?  Why?

48.  Each box of Munchy cookies contains a card of one of 4 famous baseball players.
     Assume that the boxes are randomly mixed, and that a card for each player appears in
     the same number of boxes.  Estimate the chance of getting a complete set of all four
     famous players if you buy exactly 8 boxes of Munchy cookies.

49.  A 6 cm by 12 cm by 22 cm rectangular block of wood is painted red and then cut into small cubes, each of which has a surface area of 6 square centimeters.  How many of the cubes have red paint on:
a.  exactly 1 face?          b.  exactly 2 faces?          c.  none of the faces?

50.  Find the number of revolutions per minute that the wheels of a bicycle are turning given that it is traveling at a rate of 55 feet per second, and that its tires have a diameter of 30 inches.

51.  Suppose ABCD is a rectangle with  point X an arbitrary point on side AB.
Show that  $AX^2 + CX^2 = BX^2 + DX^2$.

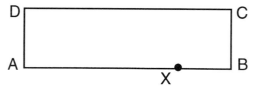

52.  A circle is inscribed inside a square and then a circle is circumscribed outside the square.  What is the ratio of the area of the inscribed circle to the area of the circumscribed circle?

53.   The average of five counting numbers is 12.  The average of 15 other counting numbers is 8.  What is the average of all 20 numbers?  Could one of the twenty numbers be 107? Explain.

54.   Prove that the distance from the midpoint M of the hypotenuse  of any right triangle ABC to each of its three vertices A, B, and C is the same.

55.   Find the measure of each angle of a regular polygon that has:

      a.  2 diagonals        b.  5 diagonals        c.  9 diagonals        d.  35 diagonals

56.   A 6-meter wide alley runs between two buildings.  In the alley are two crisscrossed ladders as shown in the diagram. If the tops of the ladders are 10 meters and 15 meters above the ground, how high is the point at which they cross?

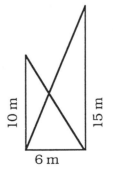

10 m   15 m

6 m

## ANSWERS TO ODD NUMBERED PROBLEMS

### Guess and Test

**1-A.** 42 meters by 68 meters

**1-1.**
| | | | |
|---|---|---|---|
| 15 | 6 | 9 | 4 |
| 10 | 3 | 16 | 5 |
| 8 | 13 | 2 | 11 |
| 1 | 12 | 7 | 14 |

**1-3.** 5 pencils and 10 erasers

### Use a Variable

**2-A.** Ken: $x$    Tom: $x+9$    Randy: $x+4$    Jill: $x+1$
$x + (x+9) + (x+4) + (x+1) = 4x +14$
$4x +14$ is even. Hence, $4x +14$ cannot equal 45.

**2-1.** 1    Denominator: $n$    Numerator: $(n+1)^2 - n(n+2) + (n-1) = n$    $n/n = 1$

**2-3.** $x$  $y$  $z$  $(x+y+z)$  $(x+2y+2z)$  $(2x+3y+4z)$  $(4x+6y+7z)$  $(7x+11y+13z)$
Sum $= 16x+24y+28z = 4(4x+6y+7z)$

### Draw a Picture

**3-A.** The ball will be 6 feet above the ground.

**3-1.** 13 correct    4 incorrect    3 with no answer

**3-3.** Box Z: 9 marbles    (Box X: 18 marbles    Box Y: 9 marbles)

### Look for a Pattern

**4-A.** Pattern of *s: $2^2 + 1$    $3^2+ (1+2)$    $4^2+ (1+2+3)$    $5^2+ (1+2+3+4)$
T is the 20th set. Thus, there are 651 *s in T.

**4-1.** a. 3    b. 7    c. 4    d. 9

**4-3.** a. $900 = 30^2$    b. 83    c. $3600 = 60^2$

## Make a List

**5-A.**  66: 22 22 22      19 19 28      19 22 25
      75: 25 25 25      28 28 19      22 25 28

**5-1.**    a.  1, 2, 3, 5, 8, 13, 21      b.  6, –5, 1, –4, –3, –7, –10
           c.  2,-1,1,0,1,1,2          d.  5, 6, 11, 17, 28, 45, 73

**5-3.**    429 (500 odd numbers less than 1,000. 142/2 = 71 are divisible by 7. 500-71 = 429)

## Solve a Simpler Problem

**6-A.**    84 rectangles

**6-1.**    130 cm$^2$      (6.5 × 20 = 130)      Small rectangle: 2.5 × 4cm

**6-3.**    The average of the missing numbers is 108. {10, 12, 14, ..., 206}
        10: Average = 10;      10, 12: Average = 11;      10, 12, 14: Average = 12.
        Hence, the 99 hidden numbers have an average of 108 (99 + 9).

## Draw a Diagram

**7-A.**    12 (Odd, Different digits, Greater than 700. Digits: 1, 2, 3, 5, 6, 7)
        713    715    721    723    725    731    735    751    753    761    763    765

**7-1.**    The 2 boys cross. One comes back. One man crosses. The other boy comes back. The 2 boys cross again. One boy comes back. The 2nd man crosses. One boy comes back. The 2 boys cross. All are now on the other side of the river.

**7-3.**    55 lines will be needed. (2 → 1    3 → 3    4 → 6    ...    11 → 55)

## Use Direct Reasoning

**8-A.**    A  B  C  →  8 6 4        D  E  F  →  2 7 0

**8-1.**    Game 1:  A, B → 3, 0  4, 1    5, 2    6, 3    7, 4    8, 5    9, 6    10, 7  11, 8
        Game 2:  A, B → 8, 9  7, 8    6, 7    5, 6    4, 5    3, 4    2, 3    1, 2    0, 1

**8-3.**    He smoked 21 cigarettes the day before he started to cut back.
        $x$        ($x - 2$  $x - 4$  $x - 6$  $x - 8$  $x - 10$  $x - 12$  $x - 14$)    $7x - 56 = 91$  $x = 21$

### Use Indirect Reasoning

**9–A.** Suppose C is even. We know that the sum of the 5 consecutive counting numbers is odd. Thus, 3 of the 5 numbers must be odd. This means that when A+C+E is odd, B+C+D must be even. Hence, A+C+E cannot equal B+C+D when C is even. Thus, C is odd.

**9–1.** The farmer used 297 posts.

**9–3.** Lincoln:76      Kennedy:84      Jefferson:38      Madison:19

### Use Properties of Numbers

**10–A.** The number is 823. ($8 \times 9 \times 11 = 792$.   Start with791. Then try 799. Then try 807. Continue until the pattern reaches 823.)

**10–1.** Jim has 27 rare coins in his collection. There were 6 cups.

**10–3.** There were 30 envelopes and 46 sheets in each box.

### Solve an Equivalent Problem

**11–A.** 120 ways ($5 \times 4 \times 3 \times 2 \times 1$)

**11–1.** The numbers are 8, 11, and 20.

**11–3.** 7 pets      2 rabbits      2 cats      3 dogs

### Work Backward

**12–A.** Pail X: 33 ounces      Pail Y: 15 ounces

**12–1.** Won/lost → A: 5/1    B: 4/2    C: 3/3    D: 0/6

**12–3.** Ten boys are 7th graders.

### Use Cases

**13–A.**

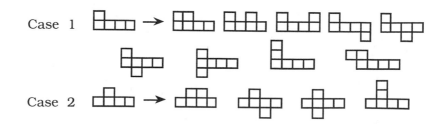

**13–1.** She bought 33 tennis balls (11 cans) and 16 racquet balls (8 cans).

**13–3.** Fridley/Alexendria, St. Cloud/Edina, Mankato/Duluth, Cambridge/Hopkins

**Solve an Equation**

**14-A.** 240 miles [$d = rt$     $5r = (24/5)(r + 2)$     $r = 48$ mph     $d = 5 \times 48 = 240$ miles]

**14-1.** 20     36     28     28     28     28

**14-3.** Jane saved $900 during that time.

**Look for a Formula**

**15-A.** a. 395,   $4n-1$     b. $2^{101}$, $2^{n+2}$     c. 9,900, $n(n+1)$

**15-1.** 4,158, $n+(n+76) = 108$     $n = 16$     16, 17, 18, ..., 92   $38 \times 107 + 92 = 4,158$

**15-3.** Train length: 0.1 mile     Tunnel length: 1.5 miles
90 miles per hour = 1.5 miles per minute = 0.1 miles in 4 seconds.

**Do a Simulation**

**16-A.** Answers will vary. The probability of winning a prize is 24/70 or about 0.34.

**16-1.** 1,800 five-digit numbers are divisible by 50.
Smallest: 10,000 = 200 × 50     Largest: 99,950 = 1,999 × 50

**16-3.** A, B, C → 8, 2, 4     D, E, F → 8, 8, 8

**Use a Model**

**17-A.** There are two possible surface areas. (16 $in^2$ and 18 $in^2$)

**17-1.** 24 of the smaller cubes will have 2 red faces and 8 will have no red faces. Each edge of the original cube was 4 units long.

**17-3.** Suppose $n$ is the largest number of feathers on any one turkey.
Number of turkeys:     1   2   3   . . . $n$    $n+1$
Number of feathers:     1   2   3   . . . $n$    $x$     $x = 1$ or 2 or 3 or . . . or $n$

**Use Dimensional Analysis**

**18-A.** One mile = 1609.344 meters. (2.54) (12) (5280)/100 meters

**18-1.** 315 people were interviewed.

**18-3.** 6 blue cubes will balance with 5 white cubes.

### Identify Subgoals

**19–A.**  Angle  ABC  has measure 31.5 degrees.

**19–1.**  Scott and Tom will be tied 1 meter from the finish line.  Scott will win the race.

**19–3.**

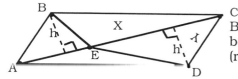

Both regions have $\overline{EC}$ as a base and both have altitude  h  to that base.  Area (region  X  or  Y) = $1/2 \cdot EC \cdot h$.

### Use Coordinates

**20–A.**  6 square units

**20–1.**  Jane's average rate was 8 miles per hour.
Total time = $(x/2)/18 + (x/3)/8 + (x/6)/3 = x/8$
Average rate = $x/(x/8) = 8$  miles per hour

**20–3.**  11 trains, counting the 1 at the start and the 1 at the end.

### Use Symmetry

**21–A.**  The first player can be a sure winner.  Start by placing a marker on the dot at the far left  (middle dot).  Then place a marker on the dot that is symmetrically opposite the one placed by your opponent, unless you can place a marker to complete a string of  3.

**21–1.**  Each angle has measure 135 degrees.  (Regular octagon)

**21–3.**  11  candy bars     $(187 = 11 \times 17$        17 cents each  $\rightarrow$  32%  off)

## ANSWERS TO ADDITIONAL PRACTICE PROBLEMS

**Guess and Test** 1. 41,472

**Use a Variable** 1. Yes. $43 + 45 + 47 + 49 + 51 + 53 + 57 = 343$

**Draw a Picture** 1. Glen is 100 meters from the starting line in the direction Leo is running.

**Look for a Pattern** 1. a. 1600 b. 179 c. 56 d. 2491

**Make a List** 1. 10 ways

**Solve a Simpler Problem** 1. a. 81 b. 181

**Draw a Diagram** 1. Two women in the class are left-handed.

**Use Direct Reasoning** 1. Ken

**Use Indirect Reasoning** 1. Suppose AB = 2BA. Then $10A+B=20B+2A$ and $8A=19B$. Impossible! Why?

**Use Properties of Numbers** 1. a. K=6 b. K = 0,2,3,5,6,8,or 9. c. k=2 or 6

**Solve an Equivalent Problem** 1. 768 ways ($3 \times 2^8 = 768$)

**Work Backward** 1. 66

**Use Cases** 1. $0 < X < Y$ or $Y < X < 0$

**Solve and Equation** 1. 10 pounds

**Look for a Formula** 1. 44,100 $(1+2+3+4+ \ldots +20)^2 = 44,100$

**Do a Simulation** 1. 0.3

**Use a Model** 1. One possible solution is: Row 1:WYBR Row 2:BRWY Row 3:RBYW Row 4:YWRB

**Use Dimensional Analysis** 1. 125

**Identify Subgoals** 1. Row 1: 22 13 16 11 Row 2: 17 10 23 12
Row 3: 15 20 9 18 Row 4: 8 19 14 21

**Use Coordinates** 1. 120 square units

**Use Symmetry** 1. A(-4, 8) B(-7, 12) C(-23, 12) D(-20, 8)

## ANSWERS TO ADDITIONAL MIXED STRATEGY PRACTICE

1. 3 inches from each edge and 3 inches between pictures

3. 31 grams (Box: 29 grams    Red Chip: 2 grams)

5. The amounts are equal

7. 18 and 36

9. 16 pencils and 7 pens

11. Ken: 12    Barb: 10    Sam: 5    Linda: 3

13. 6 nickels (12 dimes  2 quarters)  OR  1 nickel (7 dimes  5 quarters)

15. 78 rectangles (1+2+3+4+. . .+12 = 78)

17. 94 ways

19. Option B is better when 11 or more vacuum cleaners are sold per month.

21. 87178291200.  The number must end with 2 zeros and it must be divisible by 3.

23. 44

25. 18 miles (D/8 - D/24 = 3/2 $\Rightarrow$ D = 18)

27. 247 and 249

29. 21

31. 120 seconds

33. a. ▢    b. △    c. ○

35. 720 cubic inches

37. 0 1 2 3: Girls    4 5 6 7 8 9: Boys
One trial: 3 digits (e.g., 421: 2 girls, 1 boy)

39. 36 gallons

41. Each 1 x 2 rectangle must cover one ▨ square and one ▢ square.

43. Put one white ball into a box.  Then put the remaining balls into the other box.

# ANSWERS TO ADDITIONAL PRACTICE PROBLEMS

45.     Subgoal: Show why 65 must be the sum of the numbers in each row, column, and diagonal.

Indirect Reasoning: Suppose that 1, 2, 3, and 4 are all corner numbers. Impossible. Why?

47.     Prob.(X will win)=46/112    Prob.(Y will win)=58/112    Prob.(tie)=8/112

49.     a.  640 faces              b.  136 faces              c.  800 faces

51.

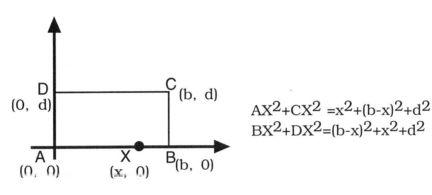

$$AX^2 + CX^2 = x^2 + (b-x)^2 + d^2$$
$$BX^2 + DX^2 = (b-x)^2 + x^2 + d^2$$

53.     Average = 9.        No!  The largest possible number is 100.

55.     a.  90°     b.  108°     c.  120°     d.  144°